Success Strategies and Knowledge Transfer
in Cross-Border Consulting Operations

Economics of Science, Technology and Innovation

VOLUME 19

Success Strategies and Knowledge Transfer in Cross-Border Consulting Operations

by

Roger Svensson
The Research Institute of Industrial Economics
Stockholm, Sweden

KLUWER ACADEMIC PUBLISHERS
Boston / Dordrecht / London

Distributors for North, Central and South America:
Kluwer Academic Publishers
101 Philip Drive
Assinippi Park
Norwell, Massachusetts 02061 USA
Telephone (781) 871-6600
Fax (781) 871-6528
E-Mail <kluwer@wkap.com>

Distributors for all other countries:
Kluwer Academic Publishers Group
Distribution Centre
Post Office Box 322
3300 AH Dordrecht, THE NETHERLANDS
Telephone 31 78 6392 392
Fax 31 78 6546 474
E-Mail <services@wkap.nl>

 Electronic Services <http://www.wkap.nl>

Library of Congress Cataloging-in-Publication Data

Svensson, Roger.
   Success strategies and knowledge transfer in cross-border consulting operations / by Roger Svensson.
      p. cm.-- (Economics of science, technology, and innovation ; 19)
      Includes bibliographical references and index.
      ISBN 0-7923-7776-1 (alk. paper)
      1. Business consultants. 2. International business enterprises--Management. I. Title. II. Series.

HD69.C6 S954 2000
658.4'6--dc21
                                        99-086381

Printed on acid-free paper. Printed in the United States of America
Printed in the United States of America

CONTENTS

Appendix

LIST OF FIGURES

LIST OF TABLES

PREFACE AND ACKNOWLEDGEMENTS

This book about cross-border consulting operations was completed at The Research Institute of Industrial Economics (IUI) in Stockholm. IUI has a long tradition of studying international trade and foreign direct investment. However, previous research has only concerned manufacturing firms, which can be partly explained by the fact that detailed data on other sectors has not been available. The purpose of this book is to analyze several issues related to the international operations of consulting firms (CFs); for example, success factors when tendering for new contracts abroad, the choice between establishing permanent offices and exporting from the home country, knowledge transfer to emerging markets when consulting projects are implemented, the role of development agencies, and the consequences of state-owned CFs competing with private CFs are some of the issues that are investigated. These issues are examined on the basis of theories about consulting firms and services. For the empirical analysis, I use a unique database on individual tender documents submitted by Swedish CFs. To the best of my knowledge, this is the most detailed database on consulting exports and the only one in the world on individual tender documents.

The book and research project were possible thanks to the executives at the Swedish CFs who spent many hours filling in hundreds of questionnaires. Among these executives, I would like to express special gratitude to Jonas Belfrage, SWECO International, and David Montgomery, Hifab International, from whom I received insightful comments and with whom I had an endless number of discussions. Constructive comments were also received from Claes Hugo, Swedish Trade Council, Per-Göran Carlsson, Ministry of Foreign Affairs, Johan Åkerblom and Johnny Andersson, Sida, and Thomas Andersson, OECD. Thanks also to the Swedish Federation of Architects and Consulting Engineers which supported the research project and persuaded its member firms to participate in the project. At IUI, the author is grateful to Pontus Braunerhjelm, Magnus Henrekson, Ulf Jakobsson, Lars Oxelheim, Lars Persson, Johan Stennek and Per Thulin for constructive suggestions. In addition, I am thankful to Elisabeth Gustafsson who helped me fit the chapters into a coherent manuscript. Finally, I would like to acknowledge generous financial support from the Marianne and Marcus Wallenberg Foundation.

Roger Svensson

November, 1999

Chapter 1

INTRODUCTION

1.1 The Consulting Sector Deserves more Attention

During the last 30 years, the importance of the private service sectors for GDP and employment has increased substantially in the industrialized world. One explanation advanced in the literature is that this change partly reflects the emergence of the knowledge-based economy that has forced manufacturing, as well as other firms, to focus on the core business to stay competitive (Wikström and Normann, 1994; Tordoir, 1995; Nielsen, 1996). These firms have thereby chosen to outsource peripheral services (e.g., marketing, cleaning and customer services) permanently to specialized service firms, or to purchase such services (e.g., management, IT and financial services) on a project basis from consulting firms (CFs). Simultaneously, the manufacturing sector has continued to rationalize and increase its productivity, implying that a substantial part of the workforce has been driven to look for employment in other sectors. This has facilitated the emergence of new services that did not exist earlier (e.g., Internet, computer and mutual fund services) and has led to a restructuring of the whole business sector. In most industrialized countries, the manufacturing sector's share of GDP and employment has decreased from a range of 40% to 50% 30 years ago to between 15% and 30% today. Even within manufacturing, many of the supplied products today are services such as contractor, training and after sales (Grönroos, 1990).

According to the United Nations (1998), the sectors outside the manufacturing industry, namely, the service, energy, telecom, wholesale and retail distribution sectors, account for more than 50% of the worldwide flow of foreign direct investment today. The growth in internationalization of the service sectors—especially the banking and finance, insurance, consulting, accounting and media sectors—is also outpacing the manufacturing sector. The relatively late internationalization stems from restrictions that prohibited foreigners from owning shares in these sectors. For exports, the impact of services is less notable. In 1995, the service sectors accounted for 20% of worldwide trade (World Bank, 1998).[1] Irrespective of the measure used, internationalization is

---

[1] In general statistical tables, service exports account for only a small part of overall exports, whereas manufacturing exports dominate for almost all countries. However, a large part of the manufacturing exports consists of services embodied in the finished goods, for example, IT,

increasing. In particular, the emergence of data and telecommunications has made it possible to export services over long distances (e.g., database and financial services).

Despite the decreasing importance of manufacturing, almost all research on international trade and foreign direct investment still focuses on this sector. The consulting sector is one of the service sectors that has expanded the most in recent years—both in the domestic and foreign markets. For example, the Swedish consulting sector has expanded by 20% annually in recent years (Lageson, 1999). In many developed countries, this sector already accounts for 5% to 10% of overall employment and output. With the exception of a book on the internationalization of professional services in general (Aharoni, 1993), little effort has been devoted to analyzing international trade in the consulting sector —in particular, no detailed empirical study exists. In this book, I examine international operations in this sector closely, both theoretically and empirically.

What are consulting services and why should they be important in international trade? Consulting means that *services are sold on a project basis* to the clients. All firms that supply services in such a manner and do not use any physical capital—either as machineries or as a means of transport—are here defined as CFs.[2] The CFs thereby offer the client flexibility, the alternative for the client being to employ professionals permanently. CFs typically gather and collect information and knowledge about technology, management, computers, statistics, laws, and so on, which are packaged and sold as services. In fact, CFs may be the prototype example of knowledge-based firms. The knowledge is embodied in the employees (also called professionals) in the form of human capital. It is therefore likely that CFs play an important role in knowledge transfer (Siggel, 1996). Furthermore, consulting services cannot be evaluated before they are purchased; that is, there might be a problem with asymmetric information where the supplier has more information about the services than the client does. Characteristic features of the consulting sectors are therefore that clients use "repeat purchases" from the same CF, and that strong confidence bonds or long-term relationships are developed between the CFs and their clients.

---

engineering, management and financial services. Therefore, service exports are underestimated.

[2] Tordoir (1995) claims that consulting must include some form of judgement. Here, I use a broader definition of consulting that includes any services that are sold on a project basis and do not require any phyical capital, e.g., engineering, IT, management, juridical, accounting, training, outplacement, marketing, and financial services. The advantages with this broader definition are that it is difficult to evaluate whether a service includes any judgement or not, and the economic theory is the same for all services sold on a project basis irrespective of whether any judgement is included or not. Services that are sold on a continuous basis like insurance, bank, security and cleaning services, or services that are permanently outsourced to separate firms are not regarded as consulting services. Furthermore, construction and transportation services that require large amounts of physical capital to produce the services are not consulting services.

One important actor in international operations is the development agencies.[3] These agencies have recently paid increasing attention to the fact that the implementation of consulting services should be associated with intensive knowledge transfer. The development agencies used to finance huge infrastructure projects, but nowadays more of their spending is directed toward purchases of consulting services. Not surprisingly, 60% to 80% of the consulting services exported from developed countries are directed to developing countries and Eastern Europe (Svensson, 1997), henceforth called "emerging markets". This pattern differs significantly from that of the international trade in goods, 70% to 80% of which takes place between developed countries (UN, 1997). Development agencies, and sometimes also government authorities, have specific rules for procurement of consulting services. The purpose of such rules, which differ from those used in the commercial market, is to minimize the problem with asymmetric information and to facilitate the choice of supplier. These rules may relate to tenders in competition, negotiations, the extent to which local firms and personnel should participate in the project, and, above all, the factors that should be given priority when purchasing consulting services.

The development agencies claim that priority is given to the skill and experience factors of the CFs and of the CFs' employees when tender documents are evaluated. Such factors are generally given a weight of 75% to 85%, whereas the price levels of the tender documents are given a weight of 15% to 25% (EFCA, 1997). A problem, however, is that the evaluation of experience and competence factors may be subjective. Not surprisingly, many CFs operating abroad also use other competitive factors and strategies in the tendering process. These factors include 1) long-term relationships with the clients (e.g., previous clients are prioritized and the CF visits the client before the tender document is submitted); and 2) local networks (e.g., establishment of offices in the host country and cooperation with local CFs). Interesting issues concern the competitive and strategic factors that generate success when tendering, and the way the rules of the development agencies affect the selection of the CF. Another interesting issue is how these rules influence the knowledge transfer to the host countries.

The increasing importance given to expertise and services is especially emphasized in the infrastructure sectors. Investment in, and restructuring of, infrastructure plants and systems (e.g., telecom systems, power plants, roads, railways and airports) are necessary for growth and development of the whole economy. Although knowledge transfer is important in both investment and

---

[3] The term development agencies includes bilateral government development agencies (e.g., Sida, Danida, NORAD) and international development banks (e.g., World Bank, AsDB, AfDB), but excludes nongovernmental organizations (e.g., the Red Cross, the World Wildlife Fund).

restructuring projects, the CFs have a central role in investment projects because they are advisors to the client when services, systems and raw materials are procured from contractors and investment material suppliers. This role is particularly important in the case of exports, because it may result in multiplier effects for contractors and investment material suppliers originating from the same country as the CF.

In addition to the trend toward more consulting services in the infrastructure projects, there is also a trend toward a larger share of management services purchased from international CFs at the expense of traditional engineering services. One reason is that local engineers in the host countries may have learned more about the technical aspects, but they do not necessarily know how to organize and plan the projects. This means that CFs in developed countries need new types of employees and competence to be competitive abroad. The extent and consequences of this shift toward management services for the CFs and the consulting sector is another issue that is highlighted in this book.

1.2 The First Book about International Consulting Operations

The aim of the book is to present a general view of CFs, the services they supply and their foreign operations in the infrastructure sectors, as well as to discuss their impact on host and home countries. I provide theoretical analysis and empirical evidence for the following issues:

1) The choice between exports from the home country and acquisition or establishment of a permanent office in the host country (Chapter 3).
2) The role, and consequences, of development agencies in the international consulting market (Chapter 4).
3) To which degree and under which conditions CFs transfer knowledge to emerging markets (Chapter 5).
4) Success factors that determine the selection of supplier when consulting services are purchased in competition and when they are negotiated. Projects financed by development agencies are compared with commercial projects (Chapter 6).
5) The growing importance and consequences of supplying management services in the infrastructure sectors (Chapter 7).
6) The consequences of that state-owned CFs operate in the international market for private CFs (Chapter 7).

Many other aspects and issues of international CFs are also discussed (for example, in Chapter 8), although in a less detailed way. All six of the issues listed should be of interest to CFs, the academic community, and other researchers; development agencies would be interested in issues 2 to 6. The clients' main interest would be in issues 2 to 5, and politico-economic decision makers would be particularly concerned with issues 2, 3, 4 and 6. These six issues about international consulting have not been examined in earlier literature. In fact, literature in this area is scarce; the reader is directed to the few relevant previous studies in the respective chapters. My objective with this book is to start a new strand of literature about the internationalization of the consulting service sectors. To my knowledge, no analytical book about cross-border consulting operations has previously been published. The few books about consulting have either analyzed CFs in the domestic market, where the focus has been on the CF's internal strategies (Løwendahl, 1997; Maula, 1999), or have examined international trade in professional services in general, where no detailed databases have been available (Aharoni, 1993).

The analysis in this book focuses on CFs and the services they supply in foreign markets, either in the form of export from the home country or as sales from permanent offices abroad. In particular, I focus on CFs that operate in the infrastructure sectors (that is, their clients are from these sectors). There are two main kinds of CFs that operate in these sectors: 1) technical consulting firms (TCFs), that is, consulting engineers, architects and quantity surveyors; and 2) management consulting firms (MCFs). The client may be a government authority, a local privately owned or state-owned infrastructure operator or a multinational infrastructure operator established in the host country. The infrastructure sectors are here defined broadly. The natural group of sectors to analyze includes transport infrastructure, telecommunication, energy, water and building, but I also include a group of environment and natural resource sectors and parts of the manufacturing sector.

There are three reasons for adding the latter group of sectors. First, CFs operating in the former sectors also tend to operate in the latter sectors (e.g., a CF that designs an industrial building will perhaps design the process system). Second, the types of services supplied in the two groups of sectors are similar (e.g., master plans, feasibility studies, procurement and supervision). Third, exact definitions of the sectors are not entirely settled. Many projects, in fact, include services in several sectors (e.g., in the water, environment and natural resource sectors). The included sectors and the extent of their services are shown in Table 1.1.[4]

Sometimes, CFs and contractors are integrated in the same firm. Such firms are not considered in this book, although much of the analysis would be relevant

---

[4] The transport infrastructure and energy sectors have been divided into subsectors because our databases are concentrated in these sectors and have many observations in them (see Appendix A).

Table 1.1. Extent and division of infrastructure sectors included in the analysis.

Sector	Sub-sector	Extent
Transport infrastructure	Roads and railways	Roads and railways
	Ports, airports and bridges	Ports, airports, bridges, tunnels and town-planning
Telecommunication		Telecommunication
Energy	Power and electricity	Power, electricity and transmission
	Hydro power	Hydro power and dams
	Heating	District heating; heating, ventilation and sanitation
Water		Water supply and waste water
Environment		Waste, recycling and environmental control
Natural resources		Geology, mining, agriculture, forestry and countryside development
Buildings		Residential blocks, industrial buildings, hospitals, hotels and offices
Manufacturing		Industrial plants and process systems (excluding product development)

for this kind of firm. Contractors are either manufacturing or construction firms. Both of them supply construction and installation services in investment projects, but the former manufacture some of the used systems and components. Moreover, CFs can be affiliated with infrastructure operators. As long as such CFs operate as independent affiliates, they are included in the analysis. Furthermore, the focus on industrial plants and process systems in the manufacturing sector implies that TCFs supplying services to product development in the manufacturing sector are excluded.

Although the analysis focuses on CFs operating abroad in the infrastructure sectors, many of the conclusions should be relevant for CFs in other sectors that are involved in foreign activities. These sectors include IT, health, education, government administration, accounting and corporate management. This applies particularly to issues 1, 2, 3, 4 and 6, presented earlier, because all CFs and consulting services—irrespective of sector of origin—have common characteristics, as I discuss in the theoretical part of the book. Some of the issues are also relevant for the sales of consulting services in the domestic market, for example, issues 4 and 6. The analysis in the book should also be relevant for construction firms, because they—like the CFs—also sell services on a project basis.

1.3 Unique Data on Tender Documents

The analysis and methodology in this book about consulting exports are based on two premises. First, the distinctive features that characterize consulting services, CFs, the market structure and the clients are examined. From these characteristics, I then develop theories and hypotheses about which strategies, actions and competitive factors are optimal for CFs to use abroad. I compare domestic and foreign operations of consulting services, as well as exports of consulting services with exports of manufactured goods.

Second, the empirical analysis relies on two unique databases of consulting exports. Both databases hold information on the foreign operations of Swedish CFs that supplied services in the infrastructure sectors during the 1990s. The first database is at the firm level and includes information about the firms' exports in relation to sectors, regions and financing, and information on the firms' foreign offices. I also have comparable data for CFs from the other Nordic countries. The second database consists of information on 458 individual tender documents (proposals) submitted abroad by Swedish CFs during the period from 1995 to 1997. Both awarded and lost tenders are included. The data covers information on the competitive factors and strategies that the CFs used when they tendered. Included are the tenderer's experience with the host country and the client, the education level and international experience of the firm's team leader, and whether the firm visited the client before the tender document was submitted. No such detailed database on service export exists anywhere else. The databases are described in detail in Appendixes A and B.

By using these databases, I then empirically test the theories about consulting services and CFs, especially the six issues mentioned earlier. Two main methods are used: 1) descriptive statistics and cross-tabulations with corresponding statistical tests when appropriate; and 2) econometric analyses where it is possible to control for several factors when testing for causality between two or more factors. In the latter case, because of the complexity of the statistical methods, I only show the reasoning and results rather than the entire statistical analysis. Reference is made to more detailed research reports.

Although the databases comprise Swedish CFs and comparisons are made with CFs from the other Nordic countries, I claim that most of the analysis and conclusions—including the six main issues—are relevant for CFs originating in other countries as well. There are, however, specific characteristics that make the Swedish case particularly interesting to study.

First, Sweden has large outflows of foreign direct investment compared with the size of the domestic market. In fact, Swedish manufacturing firms, together with firms from Holland, Switzerland and England, are the most international-ized in the world (Andersson et al., 1996). When considering suppliers of contractor services, systems and equipment to the infrastructure sectors, many Swedish firms are strong world leaders (Svensson, 1996).[5] What has the far-reaching internationalization of the Swedish manufacturing firms and contractors meant for the foreign competitiveness of the Swedish CFs?

Second, Sweden and the other Nordic countries have high taxes, a large public sector and many regulations. For example, Swedish CFs have long faced large investment and interest subsidies in the domestic infrastructure and construction sectors. Furthermore, the presence of state-owned CFs is more frequent in Sweden than in other developed countries, which reflects the large Swedish public sector. To what extent have these institutional factors had inhibiting effects on the internationalization process of the Swedish CFs?

Third, it is not sufficient only to analyze successful strategies. If one wants to learn from history, it is equally important to consider strategies that have been less successful. Here, the Swedish case is an appropriate choice. Among the Swedish CFs, there are several winners and losers that have used different strategies in their internationalization process.

Fourth, foreign operations by Swedish CFs are to a large degree financed by the Swedish International Development and Cooperation Agency (Sida), in the same way that CFs from other countries are highly dependent on their bilateral development agencies. This relationship means that, although some conclusions related to Sida may be specific for Sweden, the possibility cannot be excluded that corresponding agencies in other countries work in a similar way and also apply the same rules as Sida. The bulk of the financing of foreign assignments comes, however, from multilateral development agencies and the clients themselves, which is not specific to Sweden.

1.4 The Role of Consulting Firms and their Services

As mentioned earlier, TCFs and MCFs operate in the infrastructure sectors. TCFs provide both engineering and management services, whereas MCFs supply only management services. Engineering services are supplied in conjunction with investments, but management services are connected primarily with restructuring, although they may also be included in investment projects. My definition of CFs is, however, not strict, because few pure TCFs and MCFs exist today. Rather, most CFs are combinations of TCFs and MCFs. A client is generally the recipient of the services supplied by the CFs. It is, however, not unusual for TCFs to supply detailed design services to the contractors in

---

[5] Examples are ABB, Ericsson, Atlas Copco and Volvo Trucks.

investment projects.[6]

In an investment project, several kinds of services are supplied by CFs in five steps. The steps are, in turn: 1) master plans and feasibility studies; 2) preliminary design; 3) procurement services; 4) detailed design, project management and supervision; and 5) commissioning and training. Steps 1 to 3 belong to the *precontract phase,* before the implementation of the investment has started, whereas steps 4 and 5 are undertaken during the *implementation phase* of the investment. TCFs supply services in all five steps, whereas MCFs primarily undertake master plans, procurement services, project management and training. The services and participants included in an investment project are shown in Figure 1.1.

A master plan is a technical or economic investigation about the level of the industry, the region or the country, where basic conditions are studied to identify and plan future investment projects. Examples include transport infrastructure systems, location of manufacturing units or exploitation of natural resources. Thereafter, the CFs complete feasibility studies, which include technical and economic calculations and conditions of the investment on the basis of the client's demand, the environment at the site and the materials available. The technical tasks include where to locate the investment, how to transport materials and goods to and from the completed plant and how the environment is affected. The economic tasks are concerned with how much it would cost to implement the investment and whether there is a market for the output produced by the completed plant. Thus, a feasibility study is connected with a *specific* investment project, in contrast to the more *aggregated* master plan. The fact that master plans and feasibility studies have been done is later a necessary condition for the client to get financing for the whole investment project.

When the client or financial institutions are willing to proceed with the investment, the second step, namely, preliminary design, is begun by the TCFs. In this step, technical expertise is more dominant than in the previous step. The TCF has to decide the basic layout and design of the building, plant or system; which construction techniques, equipment and raw materials are to be used; and how to recycle water and chemicals. As a third step, the investment is advertised in international newspapers or the TCFs may suggest directly to the client a number of contractors able to implement the project. The interested contractors are informed about the basic design of the system or plant and they are then allowed to participate in the tendering process, where they may suggest their own detailed technical and financial alternatives to the investment.[7] The TCFs

---

[6] Less frequently, a development agency or another CF may be the recipient of the services.

[7] The tender systems can take the form of open, closed or staged tendering or direct negotiations between the contractor and the client. Tendering occurs whether the client purchases services from a single contractor or several subcontractors.

Figure 1.1. Flow diagram for an investment project.

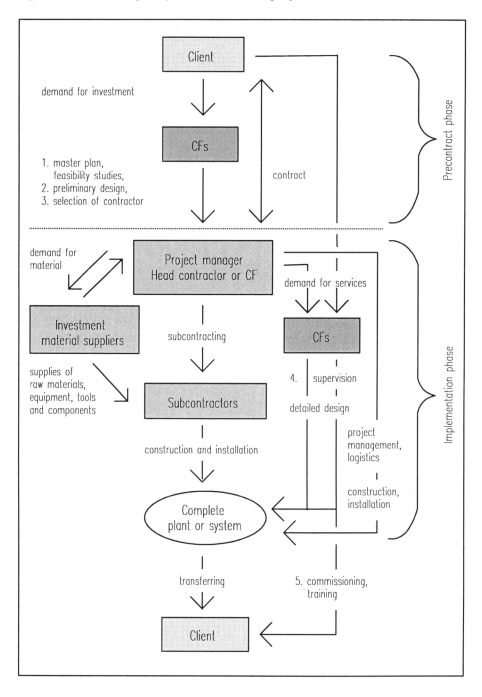

evaluate and compare the different tender documents and select the supplier(s) for the project—the contractor(s)—who signs a contract with the client.

During the implementation phase, TCFs—primarily those that did the feasibility studies and preliminary design—undertake detailed design for the client as a continuation of the preliminary design step. They also ensure that the contractor's work proceeds in accordance with costs, time limits and design specified in the contract. Occasionally, the CFs will also supply project management services and coordinate subcontractors and investment material suppliers during implementation. In this step, TCFs may supply detailed design services directly to the contractors. In the last step, the CFs train the client's personnel and commission the completed plant before it is transferred to the client. At this point, the CF may also evaluate the whole project for the client and the financial institutions.

One has to remember that the TCFs account for only a small part of an investment's total costs (5% to 10%). The large parts are supplied by contractors and investment material suppliers. As can be seen in Figure 1.1, the investment material suppliers provide components, tools, equipment and raw materials for the contractors' construction and installation, but do not do construction or installation themselves. The investment can either be a "turnkey" or "traditional" (self-administration) project. In a turnkey project, a head contractor is responsible for the whole implementation phase of the investment project. In a traditional project, the client him- or herself—with the assistance of a project management CF—leads, organizes and is responsible for purchases, logistics and supervision.[8] Different subcontractors then implement all construction and installation. Furthermore, in this situation, the TCFs that completed the studies and basic design are not allowed to supervise the contractor. However, the TCFs may still create detailed design in the implementation phase. In a traditional project, much of the detailed design is done in the precontract phase, but a head contractor takes responsibility and engages its own TCFs in this phase if a turnkey project is preferred by the client. One of the TCFs participating in the precontract phase is then designated as the "general" TCF, which is responsible for all engineering services for the client, and subcontracts different tasks to "sub-TCFs." In a traditional project, all such services are procured piecemeal by the client.

In contrast to investments where the CFs are one of several groups of suppliers, the CFs are the only suppliers of management services when restructuring is done, as can be seen in Figure 1.2. Operation services, reorganization

---

[8] A project management CF is a TCF that has mainly specialized in 1) logistics and purchasing of contractor services and investment materials and 2) supervision and evaluation of the contractors' construction and installation work.

Figure 1.2. Flow diagram for a restructuring project.

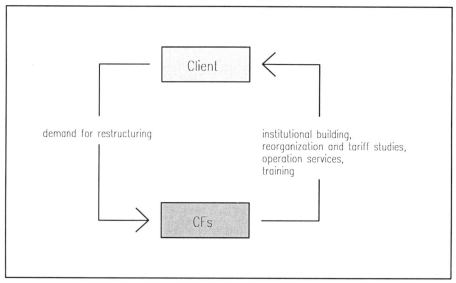

and tariff studies, and institutional building and support, as well as training and market orienting of state-owned entities are all examples of management services. Institutional building means that the CF places some of its employees with a ministry or infrastructure operator in the host country to assist with planning and management or to reorganize the institution. Many of the management services mentioned can also be supplied in connection with an investment as a sixth step after the implementation phase is completed.

In developed countries, the client would finance all investment and restructuring him- or herself. In emerging markets, the client would finance some parts, but would also be assisted by grants and loans from development agencies and loans from export credit institutes. The development agencies assist with the financing of all kinds of consulting services in either investment or restructuring projects. The large purchases of contractor services, raw materials and equipment in investment projects are financed with subsidized loans or grants from development agencies or, more often, by loans from export credit institutes.

1.5 Outline of the Book

The book is organized as follows. A general theoretical framework for CFs, their services, and the clients are discussed in Chapter 2—regardless of whether the operations are domestic or international, or in which sector the CFs operate. Issues such as the fact that the outcome of consulting services cannot be evaluated before the services have been purchased (adverse selection), that CFs are knowledge-based firms, and what kind of scale or scope economies are present in the consulting sectors are raised. What are the consequences of such features for the market structure in the consulting sector and the behavior of CFs? Standard tools of economics are used to develop theories that capture the empirically observed behavior of CFs. In Chapter 3, we then turn to the international operations of CFs. In addition to comparing exports of consulting services with domestic sales, the differences between exports of consulting services and manufactured goods are examined. Internationalization in terms of exports and foreign operation is also given a theoretical foundation. For example, the choice between exports from the home country and the establishment, or acquisition, of a local office is analyzed theoretically and empirically.

Whereas Chapter 3 deals with consulting in both developed and emerging markets, Chapter 4 discusses how the presence of bi- and multilateral development agencies affect the international operations of CFs originating in developed markets and the clients in emerging markets. For example, whether or not bilateral development agencies function as spearheads for CFs originating in the same country is tested empirically. Furthermore, the variation in procurement rules across development agencies is considered. In Chapter 5, we focus on knowledge transfer to emerging markets. The elements that must be included in the projects—training of and cooperation with local CFs and clients—for the transfer to be effective are discussed. Special attention is paid to whether or not the transferees in the host country are able to assimilate knowledge. How the inclusion of training and cooperation varies across the development level of the host country and across financing of the project is also empirically tested.

In Chapter 6, we examine empirically which strategies and competitive factors contribute to business success when proposals are submitted abroad. This issue is also tested across the financing of the project; in particular, whether or not the strict procurement rules of the development agencies are followed is tested. The analysis is done through cross-tabulations and statistical regressions and is one of the main issues in the book. In Chapter 7, the extent and consequences of the trend from engineering to management services are analyzed. Moreover, state-owned CFs are compared with private CFs and the impact of the presence of state-owned CFs on the competition in the international market is investigated. In Chapter 8, miscellaneous strategies that are applied in international markets are analyzed; for example, the choice between having permanent employees or hiring professionals on a project basis, and whether to focus on specific host countries are analyzed. In addition to considering successful strategies, typical mistakes are also presented. Furthermore, the performance in the market financed by multilateral development agencies for Swedish CFs is examined. Finally, Chapter 9 summarizes the preceding chapters.

Appendix A describes the databases and sample criteria and also provides statistics about Swedish and Nordic consulting exports from the firm and proposal data sets. Appendix B depicts the questionnaires. These appendixes are referred to continuously in the text, and can be read independently.

Chapter 2

THEORETICAL FRAMEWORK

The purpose of this chapter is to discuss the basic characteristics of consulting services, consulting firms (CFs), market structure and clients, and what these characteristics imply for the consulting sector and the behavior of CFs. As will be seen, no single characteristic of the consulting sector is unique, but the combined characteristics make this sector unique. The role and consequences of CFs as knowledge-based firms is especially examined. In principle, the theoretical framework holds for all kind of CFs. The specifics for CFs operating in the infrastructure sectors are emphasized. Attention is paid to the differences between the manufacturing and consulting service sectors. The theoretical framework is fundamental to the analysis in later chapters when I empirically describe and test various issues.

2.1 The Nature of Consulting Services: Long-Term Relationships

In many studies, researchers have tried to find characteristics that are common to all kinds of services and that exclude all kind of goods.[1] They have, however, failed to find such characteristics, because service sectors are heterogenous and products today are, to a higher degree, combined goods and services. Many goods that have a physical representation also have many services associated

---

[1] One suggested characteristic of services originated from observing the physical representation of goods and its absence in services. This distinction is, however, not always true because some services result in a physical product, for example, computer programs on diskettes as a result of programming services, or photos as a result of photographic services. Sapir (1990) states that services, in contrast to goods, must be produced and consumed at the same time. However, this argument fails in that some services can be produced long before they are consumed, for example, database services and investigation reports. Another suggested feature is that services cannot be transported. However, there are numerous exceptions, for example, financial and database services. The number of services that can be transported long distances has increased during recent years owing to the growth of information technology (IT) and telecommunications (Rada, 1987). Bergquist (1993) argues that, although a service is associated with a transaction of user rights, a good is associated with a transaction of ownership rights. This definition is valid when comparing the alternatives to hire or purchase a good, for example, an apartment or a car. There are, however, examples that do not fit this definition: photographic services produce photos and construction services result in a building that the buyers will own.

with them, for example, photos, musical compact discs and computer programs on diskette. In other words, the boundary between goods and services has become more and more blurred. Since I focus on consulting services in this book, I will try to find out the common characteristics of *consulting services*, rather than to state the difference between goods and services in general.

Consulting services cannot be stored and it is therefore difficult to test-drive them. *A basic starting point in this book is that the output of consulting services can only be evaluated after the services have been executed.* It is difficult for the client to know the quality of these services a priori—a typical "adverse selection" problem might arise because the supplier has more information than the buyer. This is also valid for some goods called "experience goods" in the industrial organization literature (Tirole, 1986), such as power plants, cars and white goods. The limited information creates uncertainty for the buyer when consulting services or experience goods are purchased that will, in turn, increase the transaction costs (Williamson, 1989). The transaction costs can be broken down into search, bargaining and control costs, which will all be higher because of this increased uncertainty. The uncertainty and transaction costs can be lowered if the supplier guarantees that the products are of a minimum quality or if confidence is established between the supplier and the buyer.

In the consulting sectors, the adverse selection problem induces the suppliers to create confidence by developing a reputation for high quality as they market their reference assignments. The CFs also market the experience and competence of their employees as a signal of the quality of services to the client. CFs that have developed a reputational capital then have an advantage compared with competitors, because they can charge a premium on the price and expand their client base at a lower cost (Scherer, 1986). The risk of failure is associated with obligations toward the client to execute services such as studies and calculations correctly. This risk requires insurance for the CFs because failures potentially put the supplier's reputation at risk, and such damage is not easy to restore. For example, when implementing investments in the infrastructure sectors, poor feasibility studies or incorrect technical and economic calculations may be very costly, partly because of the size of investment projects that may be as large as several billion dollars. This means that reputation will be an important competitive factor for technical consulting firms (TCFs) that supply such services.

Even more important, previous contracts between a CF and a client will increase the client's knowledge about the supplier and the quality of its services, meaning that historical confidence bonds or long-term relationships between the CF and client will be important in these sectors. These long-term relationships take time to develop and it is difficult for an outside supplier to break existing relationships. Thus, one can expect repeat purchases from a specific CF (Tirole, 1986). Such strong long-term relationships between buyers and sellers have also been observed by Johanson and Sharma (1983) in the technical consulting sector. The phenomenon of strong long-term relationships means that it should be particularly difficult to obtain the first contract for a client, and the CFs will primarily give priority to the needs and demands of old clients. Repeat purchases and strong long-term relationships will be especially frequent if it is costly to choose a bad supplier. That is the case in the technical consulting sector, where poor technical and economic calculations may be disastrous for an investment project, or in the corporate management sector, where bad advice about a merger or acquisition may be costly. One interesting issue is how important the signalling of firm- and employee-specific factors and the development of long-term relationships is when services are procured in the consulting sectors. This issue is empirically described and tested in Chapter 6.

In another sense, however, consulting services differ from other experience goods. Production and consumption of services can seldom be separated in space or transported over long distances.[2] Most consulting services are typical face-to-face services, because the execution of consulting services requires some form of interaction, and thereby also direct contact, between the CF and the client. Consulting services delivered as labor services—for example, training and operation services—always necessitate direct contact and sometimes cooperation when executed, whereas consulting services delivered as documents —for example, feasibility studies and design—can partly be produced at home before they are submitted to the client. Consulting services delivered as documents are, however, never standardized services, but are highly specialized and therefore require interaction between the client and CF when the project is defined and also require instructions from the CF when the completed documents are submitted to the client. Direct contact is then necessary. The direct contact can either be temporary, as occurs when the CF travels to the client or vice versa, or, permanent, as occurs when the CF sets up an office close to the client. The necessity of direct contact means that good communication, cooperation and social competence will be important—factors that are difficult to evaluate a priori. Thus, for this reason as well, one can expect repeat purchases and long-term relationships that are reinforced between the CF and the client.

After the supplier has been chosen and the contract between the CF and the client has been signed, another problem arises. The client must ensure that the CF actually supplies the services that are specified in the contract. This problem is referred to as "moral hazard" and frequently occurs when services are

---

[2] Exceptions are services that can be transported via telecommunications or the Internet, for example, financial or database services. The rapid development of the Internet and telecommunications during recent years implies that such services can be transported over long distances to a much higher degree.

executed. If developing long-term relationships with a new client is costly and difficult, the penalty will be large for the CF if he or she is caught cheating. There are then fewer incentives for the CF to cheat. In principle, the message from the client is that "if you do not cheat, there will be opportunities to buy services from you again."

2.2 The Nature of Consulting Firms

2.2.1 Independent Firms

The general reason that CFs exist as individual firms and are separated from the client can be explained by a combined efficiency and contract argument. If the client cannot employ personnel who undertake specialized services full-time because of, for example, demand fluctuations or limited need for qualified but expensive services, and such personnel have alternative uses for other firms or clients, subcontracting of these services to other firms (that is, CFs) is likely to occur. This avoids wastage of resources, and ensures efficiency for both the client and the individual professionals.[3] The presence of some market rigidity —for example, employment stoppages in the firm or authority induced by trade unions— gives incentives for the purchase of consulting services. The only way then for the firm or authority to achieve flexibility in their operations is to hire professionals, that is, to buy services from CFs. Purchasing of consulting services from separate firms may also be forced by government laws. For example, firms are required by the law to consult an independent accounting firm when assessing annual accounts.

A second reason for the existence of independent CFs is that such firms can upgrade the knowledge base among their employees at a lower cost than that if the client had employed the professionals directly. Likely there is a knowledge gap between the CF and the client. Knowledge transfer from the CF to the client is then an important part of the project. This last reason is discussed in the next section. Although the first reason is valid for all kinds of CFs (including low-skilled CFs such as Manpower Inc.), the second reason may be valid for high-skilled CFs, but not for low-skilled CFs

Another interesting point can be made about the infrastructure sectors. The explanation for TCFs being separated from the contractor stems from the client's need to involve an independent firm that selects and supervises the contractor

---

[3] For clients in emerging markets there is also a practical problem of employing specialist engineers or economists permanently, because the latter agents often originate from developed countries.

in the case of investments. This is often a requirement by the external financiers, that is, banks when investments are implemented in developed countries, and development agencies and export credit institutions when projects are implemented in emerging markets. The TCF in this sense acts as a representative of, and advisor for, the client. Sometimes, TCFs and contractors are integrated in the same firm. Such TCFs have more direct access to proprietary technologies than do independent TCFs. However, a disadvantage is that integrated TCFs are more limited in their choice of techniques because they represent the interest of the parent company. The independence of the pure TCFs may be one of the most important competitive advantages that the sector possesses, because such TCFs can choose technologies from a large number of contractors and investment material suppliers to satisfy the demand from the client (Siggel, 1986).

In principle, the CF "sells time" by hiring out its only factor of production (professionals) to the client, thereby offering the client flexibility. The CF guarantees the skill of these professionals as well as the supply of reserve professionals. The nature of this sector implies that the sales of services to a specific client is *discontinuous*. If the client needs specialized services permanently, it is cheaper to employ the professionals directly. Therefore, the CF has to sell services to many different clients and must constantly tender for new contracts, either in competition or through negotiations. The discontinuous nature of the sales make it difficult for the CFs to get full-time contracts for their employees. The CFs therefore often face situations of either over- or under-capacity, which is perhaps the largest problem for the CFs to solve. I return to this problem when analyzing the choice of entry mode later in Chapter 3, and in Chapters 7 and 8, I look more closely at how different CFs try to solve this problem either by applying a strategy of permanent employees or by hiring professionals for each project.

The long-term goal for the CF is, of course, to make profits. Some research fellows and the CFs themselves often claim that the goal for a CF is to create value for, and transfer knowledge to, the client, or that the employees or interests of the client are put first, while the firm comes second. But such goals are only intermediate goals for obtaining long-term profits. If the interests of a client are so restrictive to the behavior of the CF that it cannot earn long-term profits, the CF will not supply any services to that client. In the short term, however, a challenging project can be prioritized ahead of a high-profit project by the CF. The reason is that the former project is perhaps associated with more upgrading of knowledge for the employees and the firm will provide higher profits in the long term.[4]

---

[4] An inferior method would be to ask the CFs the purpose of their operations directly. Many CFs will then give answers other than long-term profits because they do not want to upset their clients.

2.2.2 Knowledge-Based Firms

CFs are perhaps the most pure example of knowledge-intensive firms. In principle, the only factor of production is the employed (or hired) professionals and their experiences and skills. As many as 70% to 80% of the employees in TCFs are engineers or natural scientists and the same is true for economists or engineers employed in management consulting firms (MCFs). These professionals have years of formal education, training and experience.[5] The rest of the employees are administrators and assistants.[6] The services supplied by the CFs are based on intellectual capital—either human or structural. The human capital is embodied in the employees in the form of technical, managerial and economic knowledge and skills. The structural capital (or organizationally controlled resources) is the specific experience and competence of the whole firm, such as the brand name, databases, or networks, long-term relationships with clients, or routines at the firm level. This capital is available for all employees and can be diffused and reproduced. The structural capital can be seen as traditional firm-specific competitive factors.

The long-term relationships with the clients may be firm specific, but, not unusually, they are bound to the professionals employed in the firm. This issue, is, in fact, interesting in itself, but it cannot be examined empirically in this book. Compared to "experience good" sectors, long-term relationships in the consulting sector likely are more employee specific, because consulting services are produced by the employees close to, or together with, the client. If the long-term relationships are employee specific, the CFs are vulnerable to employees who quit and bring their competitive factors in the form of human capital and long-term relationships with them. It is not easy to replace such key employees who quit. Furthermore, consulting services are nonstandardized, which means that the employees who execute the services have a large influence on the final shape of the services. For this reason and those mentioned earlier, employee-specific characteristics should be important competitive factors in the consulting sectors.

Although large investments have been made in information technology (IT) systems during the last few years, the CFs have almost no resources bound in physical capital, except for computers, software programs and these IT systems. The software programs used in the sector can be regarded as available for all CFs. Physical capital is not an entry or exit barrier for CFs, as it is for many

---

[5] The advantage with highly educated employees is, of course, that their knowledge base begins at a higher level, but, above all, that they have a faster and larger learning capacity.

[6] Manpower Inc. and other "accommodation bureaus" are the exception in being consulting firms that rely on low-skilled labor. The reason that these types of CF exist as separate firms is that they can offer flexibility to the client (see previous section).

manufacturing firms. There are, however, entry barriers in the consulting sector, which partly depend on the difficulties of developing their own, and breaking existing, long-term relationships in the market. In addition, it is not easy to recruit experienced professionals who represent human capital in the form of engineering and managerial skills, and it may also take a long time for the firm to develop a brand name.[7] However, given that some professionals employed in a CF already possess the human capital and long-term relationships with clients, it is relatively easy for them to quit this old CF and start a new CF. For this reason, key employees in the consulting sector are often offered a partnership in the firm where they are employed. They will then have fewer incentives to quit, because the value of the shares or options would likely fall if they did. By threatening to quit, key employees can raise their wages and enrich themselves at the expense of the shareholders. It is therefore not surprising that persons who are not employed in the CFs are reluctant to own shares in such firms. Large financial capital supplied by outside shareholders is in principle only necessary for the CF when it wants to acquire other firms.

The high intensity of knowledge and the fact that the CF often knows more than the client because of specialization, make it likely that some knowledge will be transferred to the client and to other CFs that are involved in the projects when the services are executed. Various aspects of knowledge transfer to emerging markets are analyzed more closely in Chapter 5. If the client learns something from the project, the CF cannot sell the same specialized services to him or her again.[8] This means that the CFs must continuously upgrade their knowledge base to stay one step ahead of the competitors and the clients. Thus, knowledge accumulates and is both the input *and* the output in the production process in the consulting sector.

The upgrading of knowledge occurs in several ways. First, the knowledge base of the employees can be increased internally by training courses and seminars or by knowledge accumulation and sharing among the employees. Second, knowledge about new and improved equipment, systems and production processes is acquired by contacts and networks with other firms like investment material suppliers and contractors, as well as with universities. Such networks are especially important for TCFs participating in investment projects to upgrade their knowledge about machineries, equipment and construction techniques, because the TCFs must guarantee the client that their recommendations will work (Johanson and Sharma, 1983; 1984). Third, hiring or recruitment of new professionals may add to the knowledge base of the firm. Last but not least,

---

[7] The consequences of that private CFs are inhibited from hiring professionals by the presence of state-owned CFs will be examined more closely in Chapter 7.

[8] An exception occurs when the client purchases consulting services only with the purpose of achieving flexibility in the demand for employees.

the most important way to acquire knowledge may be by executing projects.

The CF and its employees learn and develop existing services and techniques when new problems and clients are faced with new environments—in the literature this is referred to as "learning by doing" (Arrow, 1962; Siggel, 1985). By replicating the services for a variety of clients, the CFs are able to reduce the costs, especially in terms of time spent when executing the services. In other words, production costs decline as production experience increases. This holds for the consulting sector as long as one works with a constant technology, method or model. When the technology or model change, some of the learning effects derived from accumulated experience with the old technology or model are lost and others are retained because, in most cases, new technologies and models are largely derived from old technologies and models (Roberts, 1972). More experience also trains the CF and its employees to solve unique problems. This kind of knowledge upgrading is particularly important if each project is unique. Thus, learning by doing means that knowledge is not only transferred from the CF to the client, but also vice versa.

The improvement of services and methods when executing projects could be called research and development (R&D), with emphasis on development. This kind of R&D is directly financed by the client. Costs for traditional R&D that are not directly financed by the client may occur, but this is rare in the consulting sectors. The rule is instead that "unfinanced" R&D is undertaken by manufacturing firms, construction firms, operators and universities and that the CFs collect information about new and improved products and processes created and developed by these agents. However, when the CFs are affiliated with manufacturing or construction firms, they are more likely involved in R&D projects.

Let us return to the first method of knowledge upgrading: internal upgrading. In recent years, internal knowledge accumulation and sharing have become more prioritized. This should be important in all kinds of firms, but especially in knowledge-intensive CFs, where a large part of the knowledge base comprises human capital in the individual professionals. The problem here is to transform the human capital in a specific employee to structural capital available for all employees. In principle, there are two steps: to accumulate knowledge that individual employees have acquired and then to share this accumulated knowledge among the employees. If the CF succeeds with this transformation, the knowledge base in the firm can be used more effectively because the employees can learn from each other and reuse each others' knowledge. The time needed for routine tasks is reduced and the firms can develop and share standards and processes as consulting methodologies and task specifications. Finally, the firm will be less vulnerable to employees that quit the firm.

According to Hansen et al. (1999), a CF can choose between two different strategies when accumulating and sharing knowledge: 1) A *codification strategy* centers on the computer. New experiences and knowledge learned by individual professionals are codified and stored in databases, which then can be accessed and reused easily by anyone in the firm. Thus, the knowledge is extracted and made independent of the professional who developed it; and 2) A *personalization strategy* ties knowledge to the professional who developed it, and shares it through person-to-person contacts at face-to-face meetings, over the telephone, via videoconferences and by e-mail. Thus, personal intrafirm networks are important. The purpose of computers is then to help people contact the right person and to communicate knowledge, not to store it.

Which strategy to choose depends on the characteristics of the services (Hansen et al., 1999). The codification strategy should be chosen when the services are standardized and mature. This opens up the possibility of achieving scale in reusing knowledge. When problems to be solved are unique and services are customized and innovative, a personalization strategy is the best choice. Effective firms have been found to focus on one of the strategies (to 80%) and to use the other as a support (to 20%). For example, Andersen Consulting and Ernst & Young have applied the codification strategy, whereas McKinsey, Bain and BCG have chosen the personalization strategy.[9] In the infrastructure sectors, most projects are unique. Although many problems and tasks are recurrent, the services must always be adapted to local conditions. According to interviews with key persons in CFs in my sample, engineering and management services supplied as documents are, of course, stored in archives, but knowledge sharing is mainly done by person-to-person contacts because many services cannot be documented. A personalization strategy is thus the rule among TCFs and MCFs operating in these sectors.

Maula (1999) provides extensive and detailed descriptions of how accumulation and sharing of knowledge is tackled by large accounting and management consultants like Andersen Consulting and Ernst & Young, which have chosen a codification strategy, and how the CFs interact with their environment. Accumulation requires documentation of what the employees have experienced and learned. Nowadays, such documents are often stored in databases. A problem arises in inducing employees to spend time documenting what has been learned and contributing to the accumulation. Other difficulties are that employees use different languages and that some types of knowledge learned by the employees are not easy to document, such as the ability to solve problems or to create long-term relationships with clients, and so on. When knowledge is accumulated,

---

[9] According to Hansen et al. (1999), firms that have tightly integrated business divisions should focus only on one of the strategies. Accounting services are typical standardized and mature services. The traditional accounting consultants—such as Arthur Andersen with the affiliated Andersen Consulting, Ernst & Young and Price Waterhouse—therefore supply standardized management, juridical and IT services, and choose a codification strategy.

sharing is possible. Knowledge managers (also called human resource managers) or central knowledge teams are responsible for accumulation and distribution of knowledge among the employees in the whole firm. For example, they often hold internal training programs, arrange meetings, support the employees on how best to reuse the shared knowledge and instruct the employees on how to use the databases, and they also source external knowledge from other firms, publications and research institutes. Communication between employees in different locations and access to the databases with stored knowledge are also facilitated through Intranets. When the accumulated knowledge is accessible by the employees, it can be applied and reused in new projects, but mostly the knowledge has to be adjusted to local conditions and requirements from local clients. In other words, knowledge sharing enables the supply of repetitive services—mainly to different clients.[10]

As already mentioned in the previous section, the knowledge-sharing explanation complements why CFs exist as separate firms. If a client hires professionals from a separate firm, these professionals may upgrade their human capital at a lower cost through knowledge sharing with similar professionals employed in this separate firm than if they were employed directly by the client who does not have similar professionals in-house. In such a case, the client not only buys the executed services, but is especially interested in sourcing knowledge from the CF. This explanation for the existence of separate service firms holds both for CFs that sell services in a discrete way and for permanent outsourcing of knowledge-intensive services to separate service firms in general. In other words, the existence of knowledge-intensive service firms may be more effective than having professionals in-house.

According to Løwendahl (1997), the CFs can either base their competitiveness on 1) resources controlled by individuals or teams (human capital), or 2) organizationally controlled resources (structural capital). She suggests that the former kind of CF (e.g., TCFs, or management consultants like BCG and McKinsey) have a strategy for solving unique problems for the client, whereas the latter type of CF (e.g., accounting and management consultants like Ernst & Young and Andersen Consulting) focus on adaptation of premade solutions. In the real world, such pure examples of either type of CF seldom exist. Most CFs base their competitiveness on both human and structural capital. I claim, however, that the long-term relationships with clients and knowledge upgrading discussed previously are important irrespective of whether the CF bases its skills on human or structural capital. The long-term relationships are, however,

---

[10] An exception is inexpensive, low-skilled consulting services that can be supplied repeatedly to the same client. The client in this case is only interested in obtaining flexibility in the demand for labor.

handled by different people in the two kinds of CFs. In CFs that base their competitiveness on human capital, contacts with clients are often controlled by individual professionals, but senior managers hold the contacts with the clients in CFs that base their competitiveness on structural capital.

The fact that knowledge is transferred in both directions when projects are conducted may create a significant problem for the client. Knowledge is transferred from the client via the CF to another client that may be a competitor. This means that the client will be reluctant to purchase services from CFs or other firms in the principal area of the client's operation. The client will in this area prefer professionals in-house.

If the knowledge gap is large between the CF and the client because CFs are specialized firms, other larger problems—partly associated with adverse selection and moral hazard, as discussed in Section 2.1—arise. Since the client is then neither able to identify problems to be solved nor able to control the CF, the CF tries to sell services that the client does not need or tries to cheat the client when executing the services. It may even be difficult for the client to evaluate the services after they have been executed. To avoid this problem, the client can, temporarily, hire a professional within the same area of expertise as the CF who can identify projects and also control the CF and the executed services. Løwendahl (1997) asserts that the control problem created by the knowledge gap is the reason that society accepts professional associations taking charge of peer reviews and sanctioning inappropriate behavior. CFs present themselves as unique and have no incentives to make their services comparable with the competitors' services. By doing so, they hope to charge a higher price. This is a problem for the clients because consulting services cannot be evaluated a priori and cannot even be evaluated afterwards if the knowledge gap is large between the CF and the client.

2.3 The Market Structure: Scope Economies

Since costs for R&D and physical capital are relatively small, there are not many fixed costs at the firm level in the consulting sectors. Other fixed costs such as costs for administration are also of a modest size. Marketing is primarily directed through representation in the consulting sectors where the CFs visit the clients. This cost will thus be variable and depends on the number of (potential) clients. The development of a brand name for reputation is achieved by executing projects that can be used as reference assignments. This is a typical experience factor of the whole firm and is not developed through marketing, as is done by many firms that produce consumer goods. In international consulting, there may be office and learning costs that can be considered as fixed costs, as discussed in Chapters 3 and 4. All in all, however, there are limited economies of scale in the consulting sector. If the CF can transform human capital to structural capital and the employees can learn from each other, then large CFs will have a competitive advantage compared with small CFs. Each person can, however, only interact with a limited number of colleagues and read a limited number of documents. Thus, I expect that this scale economy effect is also of limited size.

The consulting sectors are instead characterized by *economies of scope* (also called diversifying advantages). There are *fixed costs associated with a specific project or client*. It is advantageous to sell many different services to a specific project or client, because the supplier can then spread the fixed costs across a larger sales volume. Fixed costs associated with a client or project can take the form of information, travel or contract costs. For example, a CF that has produced a master plan has an information advantage about the project and the client's needs compared with the competitors when a feasibility study is implemented. When an employee travels to a client, it is more effective to let the employee supply several services to spread a larger sales volume across the fixed travel costs. One of the most important fixed costs associated with a client is developing the client's confidence in the CF in a long-term relationship. It is especially costly to obtain the first contract for a specific client. Once the CF has established a long-term relationship with a client, the CF ideally supplies a wide range of services to the client, either in a single project or in different succeeding projects.

A given individual can execute a limited number of services and all individuals possess different skills and experiences. Large CFs with many employees are therefore able to supply many different kinds of services and can use scope economies. Scope economies explain why large firms that have competitive advantages may exist, although there are few scale economies.[11] The competition for large projects is strong because it is in the execution of such projects where scope economies can be applied.

It may also be optimal from the client's point of view to purchase all services from one supplier, that is, from a "one-stop shop," or at least let one supplier be responsible for the project. The client saves contract costs and then knows who is responsible if failures occur. Furthermore, the hourly debited prices can be reduced as each CF is offered a larger number of hours by the client. The scope economies and "one-stop-shop" arguments lead to a polarization of the consulting sector, where large and small CFs exist at the same time and partly operate in different segments of the market. Large CFs supply services to both

---

[11] CFs often have many subdivisions as well as several offices that are spread out locally—a typical feature for sectors with economies of scope.

large and small clients and projects, whereas small CFs supply services to small clients and projects. For small clients and projects, large CFs have, therefore, no decisive advantage because they cannot use scope economies. Small CFs may supply services to large clients as the exception when CFs are extremely specialized and have a unique competence that the large CFs do not have in-house. Thus, in the consulting sectors, client or project size is connected with the size of the CF.

In the infrastructure sectors, most TCFs and MCFs have between 1 and 100 employees, but TCFs with up to 2500 employees, and MCFs with up to 800 employees, are not unusual. This difference in maximum size between TCFs and MCFs is likely explained by the fact that there are a larger number of different engineering services included in an investment project compared with the number of management services in a restructuring project. Both groups of CFs are, however, small in relation to the whole market —also in specific fields of the market—and control only a few percent in market shares. Oligopolistic market structures are, in other words, seldom observed in these sectors.

An interesting perspective of the size distribution among CFs is the accounting consulting sector. The largest accountants (e.g., Arthur Andersen, Price Waterhouse and Ernst & Young) can have as many as 60,000 to 70,000 employees. These CFs have grown rapidly in size during recent years, primarily through mergers and acquisitions, and have internationalized worldwide. Two explanations are usually offered for this trend. First, the accounting consultants have diversified and today supply more services to use scope economies. Previously, they only supplied accounting services, but nowadays they also supply management, financial and even IT services. Therefore, they can spread fixed costs for a specific client across a larger sales volume.

Second, the accountants' most important clients—the large multinational manufacturing firms—have changed their organizations. Fifteen years ago, the clients were organized in geographical divisions. Each division could have its own local accounting consultant. Today, the multinational clients are organized in worldwide business divisions. A division now requires the same accountant for all of its worldwide subsidiaries. The largest accountants have been forced to follow their clients and have internationalized by establishing or acquiring offices in almost all countries. They have thereby grown extremely large. Smaller accountants that only have medium-sized and small clients have not been forced to go abroad in the same way. There has therefore been a polarization of the accountant sector. In contrast to the accountants' market, the infrastructure sectors have long been regulated and international clients have up to now seldom existed. The CFs operating in the infrastructure sectors have therefore not been forced to establish offices abroad in the same way as the accounting consultants.

2.4 The Customers: The Clients

With few exceptions, the clients of the CFs are either firms, organizations or government authorities.[12] The clients demand services from CFs because the clients, in turn, face demands from their customers for the goods, services or utilities that they supply, such as goods, telephone rentals, railway travels or electricity. The demand for consulting services is, in other words, a derived demand, and consulting services are intermediate products. One can therefore expect that consulting services will be characterized by a high degree of *customization*. The client takes the initiative on the purchase of consulting services; that is, consulting services are predemanded by the client. The rationality for a predemanded purchase is that the suppliers reduce risk and the client gets exactly what is demanded so that wastage of resources is prevented. In the case of infrastructure investments, the system or plant must be adapted to the requirements of the client, not only in terms of location, but also for output capacity. The immobility of the system or plant makes it likely that the investment is associated with sunk costs for the client, requiring detailed specifications from him or her. This ensures that the system or plant and the included services are mostly predemanded by the client (Seymour, 1987).

Because consulting services are predemanded, CFs do not spend resources on persuasive marketing. The CFs instead market the experience, reputation and reference assignments of the whole firm and the competence and experience of their employees. In advertisements, the CF presents its reference assignments or, more typically, announces the entry of a new professional or partner to the firm. But *given* that the client has decided to purchase services in a project, each CF that participates in the tender, of course, tries to affect or persuade the client when he or she selects the supplier, for example, through representation and visits.

The clients in the infrastructure sectors are operators of fixed and *immobile* plants or systems. These infrastructure plants or systems must therefore be constructed, set up or restructured on-site in the host country. When investments are implemented, the environment and other characteristics on-site must be considered, and labor, equipment, components and raw materials must be brought to the site, meaning that logistics are important.[13] These factors ensure that each infrastructure plant or system is unique. The immobility argument forces the CFs and other suppliers, such as contractors, to be mobile and to

---

[12] One exception occurs when lawyer firms sell juridical services to households.

[13] Logistics are also important in manufacturing plants, but when supplying investments on-site, the logistical problem has to be solved for every project because new suppliers, local environments and local personnel are partly combined every time.

travel to the client when producing at least some of the services in the project.[14] The clients' demand in the infrastructure sectors is characterized by a relatively high volatility, because investments and restructuring are initiated during limited time periods. This is one reason that sales by CFs are especially discontinuous in the infrastructure sectors compared with other sectors.

---

[14] As mentioned earlier, the execution of consulting services requires cooperation, which forces direct contact between the CF and the client. The client, however, only visits the CF in a few cases, for example, when the client is trained by the CF.

Chapter 3

INTERNATIONAL CONSULTING

I start this chapter by analyzing the factors that distinguish international consulting from domestic consulting. Stylized facts for international consulting are also discussed. Next, a theoretical model is presented that predicts the choice between greenfields, takeovers and exports from the home country when consulting firms (CFs) enter a foreign market. Special attention is paid to differences in foreign operations between the consulting service and manufacturing sectors. Finally, the choice of entry mode is studied empirically for CFs originating in Sweden and Denmark. This chapter examines international consulting in general, irrespective of whether it operates in developed or emerging markets; the triangular relationship between CFs, clients and development agencies in emerging markets is examined in Chapter 4.

3.1 International versus Domestic Consulting

Why internationalize? A CF decides to sell services abroad for several reasons. There may be a pull effect from clients in the home country, for example, from manufacturing firms or telecom operators that decide to go abroad. It is then natural for the client to be assisted by a CF with which it has previous experience and which it can trust. Sometimes, multinational firms wish to have the same supplier worldwide when purchasing consulting services, such as when a firm demands accounting services. The CF may then follow its clients by setting up permanent offices abroad—either greenfields or takeovers. Among the clients in the infrastructure sectors, however, internationalization is still quite modest, because these clients and their markets have become market-oriented and deregulated just recently. Another force behind internationalization is the recessions in the domestic market that may push the CF to find business opportunities abroad. Perhaps the demand for specialized consulting services simply comes from foreign clients. As the knowledge gap between developed and emerging markets still is wide, knowledge-based services are particularly high in demand in emerging markets, where local consulting is weak. Imports of services from developed countries may then be the only alternative for such clients.

Since most consulting services must be produced at the client's site, in the case of exports the employees of the international CF must travel to the host country. Service exports, compared to sales by local CFs in the host country, are therefore associated with extra expenses or reimbursements, such as travel costs for employees between home and host countries, hotel costs, subsistence allowances and establishment of temporary project offices.[1] As much as 30% to 40% of the CF's total revenues may, in fact, cover such reimbursements when exporting, as compared to 10% when selling in the domestic market (Svensson, 1997).[2] The first figure should also be compared to the transportation costs of 5% to 10% in the case of manufacturing exports. This comparison suggests that it should be more difficult to export services than to export manufactured goods.

The high reimbursements when exporting consulting services imply that international CFs—compared to local ones—must own or control some firm-specific advantage that is more profitable to internalize than to sell or license to local CFs.[3] In my view, superior technological and organizational expertise and knowledge, as well as long-term relationships with clients, constitute the firm-specific assets that the CF must acquire and control to gain international competitiveness. This view on firm-specific assets is in line with mainstream theories about multinational firms in the manufacturing sector (the OLI-theory; see e.g. Dunning, 1977).[4] The firm-specific assets are, however, more temporary in nature in the consulting sector, because these assets are often bound to the employees who can quit the firm whenever they want. Furthermore, the high transportation costs make it impossible to export low-skilled services unless they are submitted via data communications and telecommunications.

The growth of data communications and telecommunications during recent years has made it possible to export services long distances without any high transportation costs. Often standardized services, such as financial, database or accounting services, can be exported via these two types of communications. In the infrastructure sectors, only design services in document form can be exported in this way. The execution of design services in connection with investment

---

[1] In general statistical tables, consulting exports account for only for a small part of overall exports, whereas manufacturing exports dominate for almost all countries. However, a large part of the manufacturing exports consists of consulting services embodied in the finished goods, for example, IT, engineering, management and financial services. These consulting services are sold by local CFs directly to the manufacturing firm. Whether the manufacturing firm sells the finished goods in the domestic or foreign market then makes no difference for the CFs. The CFs will consider such sales as domestic sales. Thus, it is only interesting to analyze international consulting when the services are sold directly to a client in another country either through exports or sales from foreign offices. This is the case when engineering and management services are supplied to clients in the infrastructure sector.

[2] These reimbursements are partly fixed and partly variable costs for the project.

[3] It is not possible to license consulting services, because the employees control the human capital but they can be hired out.

[4] In the OLI-approach, O stands for ownership, L represents location, while I denotes internalization.

projects requires, however, that the CF be present in the host country to take account of the local environment because each project is unique. Up until now, data communications have therefore had a limited influence on the export of consulting services in the infrastructure sectors.

As a result of the characteristics of the consulting sector, that is, client-led demand, high mobility and, above all, low physical capital requirements of the suppliers, it is relatively easy—given that expertise and knowledge exist and that demand in the host country exists—for the CF to enter and exit different geographical markets compared to manufacturing firms. In manufacturing, the establishment and divestment of manufacturing units require large reorganiza- tions of physical capital. Furthermore, the human capital character of the CF's services means that the services, with slight modifications, can be used in a number of ways and in a number of countries. The market peculiarity of the services is low; that is, the CF can move personnel between different markets at short notice, with minor adjustments and at a relatively low cost (Sharma and Johanson, 1987). The significant problem instead will be to create own long- term relationships, and to break already existing long-term relationships between local CFs and potential clients in the host country.

As mentioned earlier, export projects in consulting are associated with higher reimbursements than are domestic projects. Some of these reimburse- ments are project-specific fixed costs in the form of travel, information or project office costs, which either the CF or the client have to pay. International projects must then have a large contract value to spread these fixed costs out to be profitable for both the CF and the client. Not surprisingly, large CFs will be able to supply many different services to large projects and will thereby have a slight advantage compared to small CFs in the international market (scope economies). Furthermore, the large size of international projects implies that a larger proportion of them will be procured in competition as compared to domestic projects. Approximately 50% of the contracts and around 75% of the contract values of international *commercial* projects are procured in competition, whereas only 20% to 30% of domestic *commercial* contracts are exposed to competition.[5] The reason why primarily large projects are procured in competi- tion is that such procurement are likely to be associated with fixed costs for the client because detailed proposals must be evaluated and several tender proce- dures must be undertaken. This reasoning is valid in the commercial market, though there are no restrictions or limits for negotiated contracts.

Foreign projects have a higher level of risk than do domestic projects—at

---

[5] According to Tables A.8 and A.9 in Appendix A, 38 commercial contracts with a value of 208 MSEK were awarded in competition and 43 commercial contracts with a value of 67 MSEK were negotiated in the international market.

least when considering commercial projects. This is partly because international CFs face new and unknown climatic and environmental conditions at site. The institutional setting standards, laws and rules (e.g., building permission and standards) also vary across countries, which makes foreign projects more difficult to undertake. Client specifications for their plants or organizations also vary more widely. In addition, the political risk is higher, which may comprise expropriation or nationalization of firms. Furthermore, differences in financial and tax systems, together with fluctuating exchange rates, add to risk exposure. If professionally handled by the CF, however, the higher risk in foreign markets corresponds to a higher rate of return.

3.2 The Demand Shock Theory

Since the consulting sectors have their own unique combinations of characteristics it is not likely that the theories of entry mode for manufacturing firms can be applied to CFs. For CFs, I will instead start from their characteristics and their services. The purpose of establishing "permanent offices" in the consulting sector is to sell services continuously in the *local* (and probably regional) market, a situation that CFs are forced into by the often low mobility of the clients and the high reimbursements of consulting exports. This is substantially different from the manufacturing sector, where the finished goods can either be sold in the local market or exported; that is, local demand is then not necessary. An important difference between the consulting service and manufacturing sectors when acquiring firms is that CFs have generally only one factor of production: the employees. If the employees quit and either work for another firm or start a new one, the old firm risks becoming worthless. The acquiring firm must therefore be trusted by the employees in the acquired firm. The establishment of a greenfield office in the consulting sector means that an office is hired and professionals are recruited and employed. In other words, the requirements for financial capital are low. According to the firms in the sample that have established greenfield offices abroad, such offices in emerging markets are from the beginning, by and large, run by professionals from the home country; that is, these offices are a kind of "permanent export". As time goes by, however, local professionals are employed and trained and after some years these offices tend to be run by local employees.

Turning to the choice of entry strategy in foreign markets, consulting services are purchased in a noncontinuous manner. In emerging markets where there are a limited number of clients, total demand for the services of CFs will be relatively unstable and unpredictable compared to that in developed countries.[6] Combined with client-led demand, this implies that the international CF cannot ensure continuous demand for its services in a specific emerging market. Furthermore, local CFs are weak in emerging markets, which means that the main competitors will originate from other developed countries. Transportation costs (reimbursements) will not be decisive when exporting to emerging markets, because the competitors from other developed countries have the same costs.

Obviously, CFs are not likely to establish permanent offices in emerging markets where demand is unstable and unpredictable. The risk is not that of losing capital invested in a physical plant associated with sunk costs, because the establishment of a greenfield office does not require much physical or financial capital in the consulting sector. Rather, the risk is that the CF will not get full-time contracts for its employees, which can be costly. The CFs instead have their bases in developed countries, that is, in their home country, from which projects in emerging markets are planned and organized through exports. In the host country, CFs mostly establish "representative offices" to source information and to create networks with decision makers, local firms and clients, or temporary "project offices" that only exist as long as the assignment lasts. Alliances with local CFs and agents are also frequent.

Although small in relation to the whole project, assignments connected with an investment or restructuring may be large for the CF and could be seen as a demand shock in a specific emerging market for the CF. The demand shocks force the CF not only to move between different sites in a specific country but also between different markets when following demand trends.[7] The reason is that the CF needs continuity to pay for fixed costs such as number of employees and staff managers. Consequently, many different countries must be considered as potential markets for the international CF. It is not unusual that a CF with 500 to 1000 employees has assignments in 30 to 40 different countries in a specific year (Svensson, 1997). International operations require, therefore, a higher mobility for CFs than for manufacturing firms. When the contracts for a client seldom occur, as in emerging markets, it will be more difficult for the CF to maintain the long-term relationships with clients. Long-term relationships with clients in emerging markets are therefore expected to still be important but be weaker than similar relationships with clients in the domestic market of the CFs.

In developed countries where there are relatively many clients, total demand is large and relatively predictable. This opens up opportunities for the CF to

---

[6] The demand for the CF's services will, in other words, be relatively *discrete* and *unstable* at different time periods compared to the more *continuous* and *stable* demand for usual consumption goods or the after sales to completed systems or plants in the form of services and spares.

[7] This is particularly typical for the demand of consulting services in the infrastructure market.

establish permanent offices. In such countries, the competition from local CFs is fierce, and strong local long-term relationships exist that are difficult to break. Hence, acquiring a local CF, wholly or partially, is the necessary, or preferable, alternative when entering another developed country compared to establishing a greenfield office or exporting from the home country. Acquiring a local CF, practically, means acquiring long-term relationships with local clients. Furthermore, exports to other developed countries are not favored because of the high reimbursements, as mentioned earlier.

I argue here that the stability of local demand as well as the strength of local long-term relationships in the host country are essential factors for the entry strategy of CFs. These two factors are perhaps the most distinguishing characteristics of the consulting sectors. A model for the choice between takeover, greenfield, export and no entry is shown in Table 3.1. To simplify, a joint venture office can either be a greenfield or a takeover. In line with this reasoning, a *typical* emerging market is located in the upper left corner, and a *typical* developed country can be found in the lower right corner. Furthermore, it is hypothesized that it is possible to enter the market through a greenfield establishment when local demand is stable at the same time as local competition and long-term relationships are weak. On the other hand, markets characterized by instable and low demand and strong local long-term relationships should not be interesting for the international CF to enter at all.

An important notation of this model is that even though *local* long-term relationships and competition are stronger in the right column (developed countries), *overall* competition does not need to be much stronger in developed countries compared to emerging markets. The explanation is that general equilibrium effects will ensure that many CFs originating from different developed countries will try to export services to emerging markets. Thus, if five local CFs tender for a contract in a developed country, there may also be five CFs originating from different developed countries that tender for a contract in an emerging market.

There is an exception that requires particular treatment when using this model. Exports to developed countries may occur when clients from the home country or multinational clients (e.g., energy operators or manufacturing firms), which earlier have been clients of the CF at home or elsewhere, demand consulting services abroad. The international CF then has an advantage from long-term relationships compared to local CFs. Thus, one should use the left column of Table 3.1 when the client originates from the home country or when the client is a multinational firm with which the CF has had previous experience of. If foreign assignments are only seldom awarded from such clients, as in the infrastructure sectors, export is the most preferable alternative. But when the demand from such clients is more predictable and repetitive, greenfield establishment

Table 3.1. A model for the choice of entry mode strategy in foreign markets for consulting firms.

Local demand	Local competitors and local long-term relationships between CFs and clients	
	Weak	Strong
Unstable/unpredictable	Export	Neither affiliate nor export
Stable/predictable	Greenfield	Takeover

may be the best alternative. This should be the case for the demand for accounting services.

Representative offices will be established as a complementary strategy for exports in emerging markets, that is, primarily in the upper left corner of Table 3.1. Such offices do not give any direct incomes for the CF and can be seen as a host country-specific fixed cost. To be profitable, the establishment of representative offices will therefore require a high volume of sales for the CF in that specific host country. Representative offices will not, however, be dependent on continuity in demand as are permanent offices.

When considering the underlying factors that explain the export behavior of CFs in Table 3.1, it is not surprising that CFs from developed countries have not used a traditional "establishment chain" strategy when internationalizing as manufacturing firms have done. This strategy implies that, to avoid risks, the firm will enter markets that it has the most knowledge about—in the first step the neighboring countries that are similar to the domestic market. Direct export or export via a local agent is followed by the establishment of a sales affiliate and only in the last step by the establishment of a permanent producing affiliate (Johanson and Vahlne, 1977). In the consulting sectors, the strong local long-term relationships and the high reimbursements when exporting will force CFs from developed countries to start their foreign operations (exports) in emerging markets. Furthermore, it is not possible to establish sales offices in the consulting sectors, where production and sales of intangible services can seldom be separated. In principle, the only way to start the foreign operations in another developed country is to acquire a local CF or to get temporary export contracts when following an old client from the home country that goes abroad. According to Sharma and Johanson (1987), only 7% of the Swedish technical consulting firms (TCFs) started their foreign operations in a neighboring developed country, whereas more than 70% of them did it in emerging markets.

What are the advantages with local presence or contacts when applying an export strategy in emerging markets for the international CF? Since the project is implemented in the host country, environment and soil conditions at site must be taken into account when undertaking, for example, studies and design. Local

CFs and professionals often possess knowledge about such conditions. This resource motivates contacts and cooperation with local CFs for the international CF. Contacts with local CFs is a way to get information about potential projects in the host country, but the name of the local firm can also be used to gain access to local decision makers and clients as well as to local financing. Furthermore, professionals in local CFs in emerging markets are less expensive than professionals from industrialized countries. A competitive strategy could then be that the international CF implements the more complex tasks in the project, and less complex or standard tasks could be subcontracted to local CFs or engineers. The most common strategy is to have temporary alliances with local CFs, but the alternative is to own local CFs. Minority shares should be enough to raise the reliability for the international CF as a long-term cooperator.

Government authorities in emerging markets often encourage, or sometimes force, international CFs to enter partnerships with local TCFs when the former firms operate in the host country. The idea is that knowledge will be transferred from international to local CFs, which in the long run will decrease the host country's dependence on foreign firms. At the same time, local engineers are employed in connection with the investment projects.

3.3 The Entry Mode Choice by Nordic Consulting Firms

In this section, I will analyze which entry mode strategies the Swedish CFs in the sample have used when entering foreign markets and whether these strategies are in line with the suggested theory outlined in Table 3.1. Comparisons are also made with the largest Danish CFs. It was hypothesized earlier that exports will be chosen in (emerging) markets with weak long-term relationships between local CFs and clients, feeble local competition, and unstable demand, whereas takeovers will be preferred in (developed) markets where local long-term relationships and competition are strong and demand is stable and predictable. These hypotheses are supported in Table 3.2. Ninety percent of the Swedish exports are directed at emerging markets and less than 10% are directed at developed markets. Almost half of these 10% have, in fact, Swedish manufacturing firms or contractors requesting the orders. This means that, of all exports, the proportion going to developed markets, where no Swedish clients or contractors are involved, is very low (about 6%). Instead, most Swedish CFs have used a takeover strategy of local CFs in other developed markets. Acquired permanent offices account, in fact, for almost 80% of all sales in developed markets by Swedish CFs.

Table 3.2. Sales from permanent foreign offices and exports from Sweden by Swedish CFs distributed on emerging and developed markets in 1996 in MSEK.

Sales and exports	Emerging markets	Developed markets	All markets
Exports from Sweden	1,165	127	1,292
of which to Swedish clients	(53)	(50)	(103)
Sales from foreign offices	25	471	496
Foreign sales	1,190	598	1,788

Table 3.3 depicts the location of foreign permanent and representative offices of the Swedish CFs.[8] Some Swedish CFs have large permanent offices with more than 10 employees in developed markets: SCC in Norway and Finland; SWECO in Norway, Finland and Germany.[9] ÅF has minority-owned shares in large CFs in Norway, France, Spain and England, and J&W has them in Norway. In line with the theory, all of these offices are takeovers. Several Swedish CFs tried in the beginning of the 1990s to enter the German market in conjunction with the reunification. Of these CFs, only FFNS (SWECO) acquired local offices in several steps (in line with the theory), and it is also the only CF that succeeded in getting a platform in this market, though the ownership has been reduced lately. Other firms, for example, J&W and Tyréns, tried (in contrast to the theory) to establish greenfield offices or export from Sweden. The latter offices have been closed.

FVB is, in fact, the only CF in the Swedish sample that has been successful in establishing a greenfield office in a developed market. The firm has a greenfield office in Canada and has also acquired an office in the United States. These offices have around 10 employees each. FVB's success in establishing a greenfield office and obtaining a market-leading position in a developed country can be explained by the existence of weak local competition at the same time as the North American energy sector was deregulating. Hence, when its office was established, FVB faced a position similar to that shown in the lower left corner in Table 3.1. Swedtel also has a greenfield office in the United States, but it is a permanent regional office for Latin America.

The Danish CFs have applied takeover strategies in other developed countries, as shown in Table 3.4. As many as 13 acquisitions have been undertaken in such countries. The small greenfield office and the two representative offices in Belgium are probably located there to lobby the EU administration. Although there is a greenfield office in Greenland, Greenland is not considered a

---

[8] Whether a local office, either permanent or a representative, increases the probability that the CF will win an export contract is analyzed more closely in Chapter 6.

[9] For a presentation of the Swedish CFs, see Table A.1 in Appendix A.

Table 3.3. Permanent and representative offices located abroad by Swedish CFs in 1999.

Country	Swedtel	SwedPower	SWECO	Hifab	ÅF	SweRoad	SCC	J&W	VAI	Swedavia	FVB	KM
Norway			T		T(m)		T	T(m)	t			x
Finland			T		x		T	g*				
Germany			T(m)									
England					T(m)							
France					T(m)							
Spain					T(m)							
USA	g										t	
Canada											g	
Estonia			r	r				t				
Latvia			T(m)	r								
Lithuania				r					T(m)			
Russia				r			r	r	r			
Poland					g, t	g						
Brazil	g(m), x											
Colombia	G											
Ecuador			r									
Panama			r									
Honduras			r									
Dom. Rep.			r									

Table 3.3. (Continued)

Country	Swedtel	SwedPower	SWECO	Hifab	ÅF	SweRoad	SCC	J&W	VAI	Swedavia	FVB	KM
Mozamb.	g											
Tanzania		r		r								
Zambia				r								
Zimbabwe		r		r								
South Africa	r											
Tunisia							r					
Egypt			r									
UAE	r	r	r									
Bahrain			r									
Iran			r									
Yemen		r	r									
India	g(m)		r									
Pakistan			r									
Bangladesh				r								
China PR			T(m)									
Vietnam			r	r					r			
Malaysia			r									
Thailand	g	g(m) *								r		
Philippines	g		r									

Note: A lowercase letter means that the office has 10 or fewer employees and a capital letter that the office has more than 10 employees. An 'r' stands for representative office, 'T' or 't' for takeover permanent office, 'G' or 'g' for greenfield permanent office and 'x' for an office that is neither a representative nor a permanent office, but instead a laboratory or other kind of office. An 'm' in a parenthesis means that the permanent office is minority owned. Some CFs have also temporary project offices and agents abroad, but these are not shown. * indicates that the office has recently been closed down or sold off. Only firms that own foreign offices are included in the table. SWECO includes FFNS and ÅF includes ISO, although these firms did not merge until 1997 and 1998, respectively.

completely developed country. COWI's office in England is, therefore, the only pure Danish greenfield office in another developed country.

When operating in emerging markets, on the other hand, Swedish CFs almost exclusively apply an export strategy, as shown in Table 3.2. The Danish CFs apply such a strategy, too. Temporary project offices are set up in connection with a project and withdrawn when the project is completed. When export contracts become more frequent in a host country, the CFs establish representative offices in support of the export strategy to create networks with decision makers and local CFs, to develop long-term relationships with old and potential clients, and to source information about potential projects and conditions in the host country. The Swedish CFs have established as many as 34 representative offices in emerging markets to support their export strategies, whereas the largest Danish CFs have not set up such offices as frequently.[10]

Permanent offices have seldom been established in emerging markets by Swedish CFs. There are only five Swedish takeovers: VAI VA-Projekt has a large minority-owned office in Lithuania, SWECO has minority-owned offices in China PR and Latvia, and J&W and ÅF own small offices in Estonia and Poland, respectively. Concerning greenfields, SwedPower has an office in Thailand, ÅF has one in Poland, SweRoad has one in Lithuania, and Swedtel has six offices (including one in the United States that is aimed at the regional Latin American market).[11] The Danish CFs, on the other hand, have 24 permanent offices, of which 22 are greenfields. COWI and NCG especially have applied a strategy of minority-owned greenfields.

To set up permanent offices in emerging markets is a risky strategy because of the discontinuity in demand for consulting services. Markets that are heavily dependent on commercial projects, for example, South-Eastern Asia, are particularly risky places in which to have a permanent local office. In contrast, countries that rely more on assistance and loans by development agencies, for example, in Eastern Europe, are less volatile in the demand for consulting services. This dilemma became reality for SwedPower when the Asian crisis arose in 1997-98, and the firm's greenfield office is now closed with settlement costs as a consequence. Another interesting case is the telecom market in emerging markets, which can be placed in the lower left corner of Table 3.1; that is, the market is characterized by relatively stable demand and weak local long-term relationships. Establishing a greenfield office is, therefore, a correct strategy according to the theory. It is also a strategy that Swedtel has successfully applied.

---

[10] The strategy to focus on specific host countries in setting up representative offices is analyzed in more detail in Section 8.1.

[11] All of Swedtel's permanent foreign offices did not exist in 1996, meaning that Table 3.3 is not fully compatible with Table 3.2.

Table 3.4. Permanent and representative offices abroad by Danish CFs in 1999.

Country	COWI	Carl Bro	Rambøll	NCG	NIRAS
Sweden			t *	s	
Norway	T			S	
Germany	T	T	t		t *
England	g	T	T *		
Ireland		T			
Belgium	r	r	g		
Spain	T				
Greenland			T		g
USA	T				
Canada	T				
Latvia		g			
Lithuania	G	G			
Russia	r	r	r		r *
Poland	T		g *		
Czech rep.			T *		r
Albania				g(m)	
South Africa	g	r	r	g(m)	
Mozambique				g(m)	
Tanzania	G	r		g(m)	
Kenya		r			
Uganda		r		g(m)	
Zambia				g(m)	
Zimbabwe				g(m)	
Ghana			r	g(m)	
Saudi-Arabia	g(m)				
UAE	g(m)				
Bahrain	G(m)				
Qatar	g				
Oman	g(m)				
India			G(m)		
China PR	g(m)				
Vietnam		r			
Philippines	g				
Indonesia		r			

Note: A lowercase letter means that the office has 10 or fewer employees and a capital letter that the office has more than 10 employees. An 'r' stands for representative office, 'T' or 't' for takeover permanent office, 'G' or 'g' for greenfield permanent office, and 'S' or 's' for sister office. An 'm' in parenthesis means that the permanent office is minority owned. Some CFs have also temporary project offices and agents abroad, but these are not shown. * indicates that the office recently has been closed down or sold off. NCG is a constellation of three sister CFs in Denmark, Norway and Sweden. Since the Danish CF is the largest, I use NCG here for "Danish". However, all foreign offices of NCG are available for the three sister firms.

As discussed in section A.2 (Appendix A) and later in Chapter 7, the increased local competition and increased pressure on prices for engineering services, and the increased demand for management services imply that CFs from developed countries have been forced to create alliances with, and sub-contract engineering (especially design) services to, inexpensive local TCFs in emerging markets. Alliances with local TCFs on a project basis occurs most frequently, but an alternative is to strengthen these alliances by owning (at least) minority shares in local TCFs—either greenfields or takeovers. Minority shares should be enough to raise the international CF's reliability as a long-term cooperator, and ownership could be a necessary strategy if there are a limited number of local TCFs in the host country with which to cooperate. The owner-ship will then guarantee that the firm has a local TCF to cooperate with in the host country, which also obstructs other international CFs in working with these local TCFs. Minority shares are preferred because of the high risk with permanent offices in emerging markets as local demand fluctuates. Furthermore, if the professionals employed in the local office own the majority of the shares, then they have more incentives to work harder to win contracts on their own.

The purpose of the minority-owned offices of VAI VA-Projekt in Lithuania, SWECO in Latvia and SwedPower in Thailand has been to use them in combi-nation with exports from Sweden and to establish long-term cooperation at the same time as competitors from other developed countries are partly locked out. Bulk design services are subcontracted to professionals employed in the local offices, and more complex services are executed by staff from the home country. The Danish CFs have also applied this strategy. Although there are examples of permanent offices in emerging markets that have not been used in combination with exports from Sweden (J&W in Estonia and ÅF in Poland), there seems to be a significant difference between permanent offices set up in developed and emerging markets. Whereas the former operate independently of home country exports, the latter are used in combination with these exports.

When the client originates from Sweden in the form of a manufacturing firm or contractor, Swedish CFs have consistently used the export strategy—irrespec-tive of whether the host country is a developed or emerging market. As was suggested in the previous section, a Swedish client means that the CF probably already has strong long-term relationships with the client compared to local CFs; that is, the left column of Table 3.1 should be applied. Furthermore, assignments for Swedish clients that invest in a plant or system have mostly been temporary in nature, implying that demand is unstable. Accordingly, the upper left corner of Table 3.1 is the appropriate cell and export is then the correct strategy.

I claim that the model can also be used for CFs operating in sectors other than the infrastructure. In 1994 Caran, a Swedish TCF that supplies engineering services to product and process development in manufacturing firms, established a greenfield office in England. Before the establishment, Caran had earlier exported services to affiliates of Swedish firms located in England. These manufacturing affiliates were permanently operating in England. Since there are many competent local TCFs in England, an export strategy would in the long run have led to Caran losing the clients to local British CFs, as a result of the high transportation costs. Thus, the lower cell of the left column in Table 3.1 is an appropriate choice. Although Caran already had strong long-term relationships with the Swedish affiliates, it took a long time to establish long-term relationships with local British clients. Today, Caran's office in England has around 30 employees. Had it not been for the old long-term relationships with Swedish clients located in England, a takeover strategy would have been necessary to get a platform in the market.

3.4 Summary

In this chapter, I analyzed the entry mode choice when CFs operate in foreign markets. It is hypothesized that the stability of local demand and the strength of local long-term relationships and local CFs are the two key factors that determine the entry mode choice in consulting sectors. High reimbursements will inhibit CFs from exporting to developed countries where local CFs are highly competitive and long-term relationships between local CFs and clients are strong. Establishment of greenfield offices in such markets is not recommended because of the strong local long-term relationships. Thus, acquisition is the only profitable alternative when entering a developed market. In emerging markets where local competitiveness and long-term relationships are weak, export seems to be an appropriate strategy. Since the competitors from other developed countries also have high reimbursement costs, these costs are not as important in this situation. However, the number of clients are few in emerging markets, meaning that demand will be unstable and unpredictable. The CFs that export from developed countries are therefore forced to move from one project to another in different emerging markets when following the sector-specific demand shocks. Establishment of permanent offices in emerging markets is therefore a risky strategy.

The empirical analysis of Swedish and Danish CFs strongly supports the view that developed markets with relatively stable demand and strong local CFs are entered by acquiring local CFs, whereas emerging markets where local demand is unstable and local CFs are weak will be supplied through exports. Exporting to developed markets is possible as an exception if the orders come from a manufacturing firm or contractor from the home country that operates in the local market. In emerging markets, on the other hand, representative offices are often set up to support the export strategy. Such an office can be seen as a host country-specific fixed cost and requires therefore that the CF has a large volume of sales in that host country over which to spread the fixed costs. Furthermore, there is a significant difference between permanent offices established in developed markets and the few permanent offices set up in emerging markets. The former offices operate independent of exports, whereas most of the latter offices are used in combination with exports from the home country. Because the pressure on prices for engineering services has increased during recent years, such services are subcontracted either to independent local offices or to the CF's own local offices in emerging markets, and the more complex tasks are implemented by professionals from the home country. Finally, an interesting exception to the general pattern of entry mode is the telecom sector in emerging markets. Here, local demand is stable and local competition is weak, meaning that setting up greenfields should be a appropriate strategy. Empirically, this strategy has also been applied by Swedtel, which operates in the telecom sector.

Chapter 4

DEVELOPMENT AGENCIES, CLIENTS AND CONSULTING FIRMS

In this chapter, I examine the triangular relationship between consulting firms (CFs), clients and development agencies.[1] First, I analyze the consequences for CFs and clients when development agencies finance consulting projects in emerging markets. Second, I focus specifically on the role of bilateral development agencies and how these agencies differ from the multilateral development agencies.[2] Finally, I discuss the different procurement rules applied by the most important multilateral development agencies and how these rules affect the CFs. This information will be used in the analysis in later chapters.

4.1 The Role of Development Agencies

One role of the development agencies when purchasing or financing consulting services is, of course, to assist the cooperating partner (client) in the host country. The services implemented by the CFs will have value in themselves for the clients and will thereby increase the welfare of the host countries. However, emerging markets lag behind developed markets above all in knowledge and human capital. The main reason that development agencies nowadays focus more on procurement of consulting services than on financing huge infrastructure (turnkey) projects is that they wish to facilitate knowledge transfer to emerging markets. Since CFs are among the most knowledge-intensive firms and since production of consulting services often requires direct contact and cooperation between the seller and buyer, it is then expected that the knowledge transfer will be more intensive when production occurs than it would be in other sectors. The idea is that the transferees in the host country will learn to replicate services implemented by the international CFs and that the execution of consulting services will lead to something sustainable in the host country, which will continue when the international CFs have completed their tasks. In other words, the financing of consulting services for the emerging market by development

---

[1] The term development agencies includes both bilateral government development agencies (e.g., Sida, Danida, NORAD) and international development banks (e.g., World Bank, AsDB, AfDB), but excludes nongovernmental organizations (e.g., the Red Cross, the World Wildlife Fund).

[2] I do not, however, analyze whether or not it is effective to have development assistance.

agencies can be seen as an aid to helping oneself. The analysis about consulting firms as the transferor of knowledge is further discussed in Chapter 5.

The large knowledge gap between CFs from developed countries and clients in emerging markets will cause some problems. Since clients in emerging markets, compared with clients in developed markets, will have less knowledge about the value of the services, the purchase of consulting services will be sub-optimal (Roberts, 1972). Sometimes, the clients in emerging markets cannot even evaluate the services after they have been implemented. Furthermore, such clients are seldom able to identify necessary and interesting projects and some-times cannot control whether the CFs have actually fulfilled what is said in the contract when the services are executed. It is then likely that the CFs will suggest projects that are more profitable for themselves than for the client or will try to sell services that the client does not need. The development agencies play an important role when they identify projects, assist in the negotiations and evaluate services executed by CFs, because these agencies have professionals in-house who can conduct such tasks. This is one of the main reasons that development agencies do not give assistance or loans directly to the clients in emerging markets.[3]

From the point of view of international CFs, development agencies have several functions. First, clients in emerging markets often have a low financial credibility. If development agencies assist with the financing, then the risk for the CF that the client will fail to pay for the implemented services is reduced. Projects that are financed by development agencies are therefore more attractive for the CFs and more CFs will try to participate in the tender process compared with what happens when the client finances the project.

Second, financing in the form of assistance or loans by development agencies means that the consulting services are subsidized. Normally, such subsidies are shared between the seller and the buyer, according to economic theory. Since projects financed by development agencies mostly are procured in competition with many CFs and the development agencies assist the client in the negotiations, it is likely that the client will assimilate the largest part of this subsidy. The subsidy implies, however, that CFs from developed countries will be awarded more contracts and supply a larger share of all services in a project compared with projects that are financed solely by the client in the host country. This does not mean that international CFs will get contracts at the expense of local CFs, because the project would perhaps not have been undertaken at all if the development agencies had not assisted with financing. As can be seen in Figure A.2 in Appendix A, development agencies account for as much as 50%

---

[3] Another reason is that the clients in emerging markets—especially if they are government authorities—often are corrupt.

to 90% of the financing of the Nordic CFs' contracts in emerging markets. These agencies undoubtedly play an important financing role.

Third, the involvement of development agencies may also affect the CF's decision to establish offices in emerging markets (see the analysis in Chapter 3). Since the CF can get a larger sales volume in emerging markets, it will be easier for the CF to cover fixed costs associated with a specific host country and thereby to establish representative offices. Overall demand for consulting services in a host country is also likely to become more stable when development agencies are involved, meaning that the establishment of permanent offices in emerging markets will be a less risky entry strategy.

Fourth, the international CFs may use the development agencies as a source of information about potential projects and as a market observer. As mentioned in Chapter 3, sector-specific demand shocks force the international CF to sell services to, and observe, many different markets. Since the CF is relatively small with limited financial resources, information about and observation of these markets will be a problem. In contrast to the home country, where the CF usually has several offices scattered to serve and observe local parts of the market, few permanent consulting offices are located abroad because of the sector-specific demand shocks (see Tables 3.3-3.4). Information seeking can be done either through networks or local presence such as: 1) the CF's own local representative or permanent offices, or contacts with previous clients; 2) "consortiums" and networks with other international CFs or "alliances" with local CFs and contact persons;[4] 3) networks with contractors where a technical consulting firm (TCF) may be a member in a "group" of suppliers; 4) government authorities (e.g., Ministry of Foreign Affairs) and private organizations (e.g., trade councils) in the home country; or 5) development agencies (Johanson and Sharma, 1983). In Svensson (1997), it was found that development agencies represent one-third of the market observation of potential projects abroad for Swedish CFs. Another third of the market observation is done by the local permanent and representative offices of CFs and by contacts with old clients. The rest of the market observation is made through contacts with the Swedish Trade Council and the Ministry for Foreign Affairs, or through networks and alliances with contractors as well as with international and local CFs. The information sourcing role of the development agencies is not insignificant for the international CFs. However, the financing role is undoubtedly the most important one.

---

[4] In a consortium, the participating CFs will pool their resources and behave like a single CF.

4.2 Bilateral versus Multilateral Development Agencies

The procurement of consulting services is tied assistance in the bilateral development agencies' programs, meaning that only CFs originating in the home country of these agencies are allowed to participate in the tender process (Taxell, 1996). Accordingly, there are fewer tenderers and the competition is weaker in projects financed by bilateral development agencies than in those financed by multilateral agencies. In developed countries, the bilateral development agencies in Sweden, Switzerland and the Netherlands are the most liberal in allowing foreign CFs to participate in the tender process (Taxell, 1996). In the Swedish case, foreign CFs are sometimes invited and allowed to tender for projects financed by the Swedish International Development and Cooperation Agency (Sida) and they are also awarded contracts. A problem is that Swedish CFs are seldom allowed to tender for contracts financed by bilateral development agencies in other countries. This fact will disfavor the Swedish CFs and distort the competition in the international consulting market. One should not blame Sida for this, however, but rather the protectionistic policies of the other bilateral development agencies. In Table 4.3, we return to the discussion of the share of consulting services procured from foreign CFs and the overall shares of tied and untied assistance financed by bilateral development agencies.

Apart from the function of development agencies discussed in the previous section, bilateral development agencies often try to advocate that the resources spent on bilateral development assistance in combination with a protectionistic policy will gain the donor country. If firms from the home country are awarded contracts, there will, of course, be a reflow of incomes. The knowledge base in the home country will also be upgraded as the CFs and their employees gain more and new experiences of unique projects in the host countries (learning by doing). One of the most frequently emphasized arguments by bilateral development agencies is, however, the spearhead function. The first contract a CF wins in a host country or for a specific client is often financed by the domestic bilateral development agency. Awarded bilateral assistance contracts may therefore act as spearheads for further contracts in the host countries, either financed by multilateral development agencies or by the client (commercial projects). It is, however, not equally obvious that assignments financed by multilateral development agencies are used as spearheads for further commercial projects, because the most competition is fiercer in multilateral projects than it is in commercial projects. In some cases, it may be easier to win a commercial contract directly rather than trying to win a multilateral contract and the commercial contracts thereafter.

In Table 4.1, the awarded contracts in the Swedish sample are distributed across different financing groups: Sida, EU funds, other multilateral develop-

Table 4.1. Awarded contracts in the whole sample and when the CF has no previous experience with the host country or the client across financing groups in number and percent.

| Financing group | Awarded contracts | | | | | |
| | In the whole sample | | When the CF has no previous experience with the host country | | When the CF has no previous experience with the client | |
	Number	%	Number	%	Number	%
Sida	89	39	23	45	51	52
EU funds	12	5	4	8	7	7
Other MDAs	47	21	11	22	23	23
Commercial	79	35	13	25	18	18
Total	227	100	51	100	99	100

Note: MDAs = multilateral development agencies.

ment agencies and commercial projects. Here, Sida accounts for 39% of all awarded contracts. This percentage increases to 45% for host countries with which the CFs have no previous experience. When the CFs are awarded contracts for new clients, Sida's share is as high as 52%. Thus, it seems Sida plays a significant role for the Swedish CFs when they penetrate new host countries, but an even more important role when contracts for new clients are awarded.

In Table 4.2, awarded contracts in host countries with which the CFs have previous experience are distributed by old and new clients. Of these contracts 68% are signed with previous clients. The percentages of previous clients are especially high in the other multilateral and commercial groups. In line with the hypothesis, these data indicate that a first contract (which is likely a Sida contract) will lead to future contracts financed by EU funds, by other multilateral development agencies or by the client for previous rather than new clients in that specific host country. Contracts for new clients in such host countries are instead financed by Sida, which represents as much as 50% of the contracts for new clients (28 of 56). Thus, it is hypothesized that previous experience with a host country would not automatically be followed by future contracts with new clients in that host country; rather, previous experience would primarily provide future contracts with previous clients. In other words, the experience of the client seems to be more important than the experience of the host country when the CF tenders for new contracts.[5]

There is another feature of Sida's procurement procedures that does not

---

[5] The determinants behind the selection of a supplier in tender evaluations—experience of the host country and client—are examined in more detail in Chapter 6.

Table 4.2. Awarded contracts in host countries with which the CF has previous experience distributed on new and old clients in number and percent.

Financing group	Awarded contracts in host countries with which the CF has previous experience						Percentage of old clients
	Old clients		New clients		All		
	Number	%	Number	%	Number	%	
Sida	38	32	28	50	66	38	58
EU funds	5	4	3	5	8	4	62
Other MDAs	24	20	12	22	36	20	67
Commercial	53	44	13	23	66	38	80
Total	120	100	56	100	176	100	68

Note: MDAs = multilateral development agencies.

occur when multilateral development agencies are involved. Sida purchases many services from other government authorities and nongovernmental organizations (NGOs) in Sweden without competition. The idea is that the client's corresponding organization/authority in the donor country will be the ideal implementing organization for the project, which is called the sister-to-sister model.[6] The purchases of services from government authorities sometimes concerns relatively large projects of 3 MSEK to 15 MSEK each, where the NGO or government authority is directly asked by Sida to conduct tasks in an international project (Sida, 1999a). Private firms are not allowed to tender even if they have the required qualifications, and the specifications from the invited government authority or NGO are mostly less detailed than that in tender documents submitted to tender evaluations in competition. Sida does not call this phenomenon a procurement of consulting services, but instead, "cooperation projects" with other government authorities. This is legal according to Swedish law, because all government authorities (including Sida) are considered to be in the same juridical institution in Sweden.

It is, however, not likely an optimal situation to procure such large packages of services without competition, and Sida can hardly get the best proposal by asking a single authority, which may not be cost effective. This is a typical waste of taxpayers' money, which finances Sida's budget. It is also a waste of resources in another sense. The government authorities that are awarded such contracts are financed through taxes and have no intention of exporting services in the long run. The fact that the authorities implement some projects financed

---

[6] Although Sida has evaluated sister-to-sister projects after they have been completed, it has not evaluated or considered the private alternatives to procuring services directly from government authorities.

by Sida is evidence that they have an overcapacity of employees.[7] If the government authorities do have intentions of operating abroad, it is not likely that they will win contracts financed by multilateral development agencies or the client in international competition, because they have not learned how to tender in competition when Sida is the financier. The Sida contracts could more efficiently be used as reference assignments by private CFs when they tender for projects financed by multilateral development agencies or the client. The advantages for government authorites to sell consulting services abroad are that they get some flexibility in their operations and that the competence of their employees is upgraded. These advantages can also be achieved if the authorities let private CFs administrate, and tender for, the foreign projects. The risk to lose tenders and the costs for marketing and to learn procurement rules of different development agencies are then transferred to the private CFs.

However, the occurrence of natural disasters is of course the exception— Sida is then clearly motivated to procure services directly from other government authorities. Aid must be supplied to the disaster area within a few days and there is no time to invite firms for tendering. On the other hand, this disaster assistance is only a small part of Sida's negotiated contracts with Swedish government authorities. Ironically, the Swedish government authority, the Swedish National Audit Office (RRV), whose task is to control operations and procurements of Sida and other government authorities, is one of the authorities that has been awarded negotiated contracts financed by Sida! In 1998, the contract values of Sida projects implemented by RRV were about 10 MSEK (Sida, 1999a). This fact means that the role of RRV as controller can be questioned.

The total Swedish budget for development assistance was 12.5 billion SEK in 1998. Of this, around 5 billion SEK was transferred directly to multilateral development agencies like the World Bank, the regional development banks, the United Nations and so forth. Thus, 7.5 billion SEK was administered by Sida. Sida's budget in 1998, distributed by implementing organizations, is shown in Table 4.3. As much as 3.6 billion SEK or 48% of Sida's budget was for untied assistance and was transferred to departments of multilateral development agencies and intergovernmental organizations, foreign universities, international NGOs, foreign CFs and the client directly.

For Table 4.3, I am most interested in the procurement of consulting services. The first three groups of implementing organizations in the table, private CFs and individuals, foreign CFs, and state-owned CFs and government authorities can be regarded as organizations that only supply consulting services. These groups accounted for 1.6 billion SEK in 1998. But some of the purchases from NGOs are consulting services. If we assume that 1 billion SEK (a low

---

[7] This argument does not hold for the Swedish NGOs, however.

Table 4.3. Sida's and Danida's budget in 1998 distributed on implementing organizations in MSEK, MDKK and percent.

Implementing organization	Sida		Danida	
	MSEK	%	MDKK	%
Swedish (Danish) private CFs and individuals	903	12	c 601	10
Private CFs in the sample	(386)	(5)	---	---
Other private CFs and individuals	(517)	(7)	---	---
Foreign consulting firms	46	1	c 40	1
Swedish (Danish) state-owned CFs and government authorities	649	8	n.a.	n.a.
State-owned CFs in the sample	(85)	(1)	---	---
Other state-owned CFs	(100)	(1)	---	---
Government and local authorities	(464)	(6)	---	---
Swedish (Danish) NGOs	1,693	22	991	17
International NGOs	678	9	n.a.	n.a.
Swedish (Danish) contractors and manufacturing firms	156	2	1,068	18
Swedish (Danish) public and private universities	291	4	60	1
International public and private universities	136	2		
Sida (Danida) departments or administration	214	3	551	9
Sub-divisions of MDAs	1,152	15	n.a.	n.a.
Intergovernmental organizations	342	5	n.a.	n.a.
Clients in the host country	1,272	17	n.a.	n.a.
Total budget of Sida (Danida) 1998	7,532	100	5,972	100
Direct to MDAs	5,000	---	4,700	---
Total budget for development assistance 1998	12,532	---	10,672	---

Note: n.a. = not available. MDAs = multilateral development agencies. NGOs = nongovernmental organizations. *Source*: Sida (1999) and Danida (1998).

estimate) of the purchases from NGOs are consulting services, then Sida purchased a total amount of consulting services of at least 2.6 billion SEK in 1998, that is, around one-third of Sida's total budget. This proportion is increasing. Furthermore, 1.3 billion SEK of Sida's budget is paid directly to the clients in the host countries, who are allowed to procure goods and services themselves. An unknown amount of this 1.3 billion SEK is for consulting services. However, it is not likely that more than 1 billion SEK of the overall consulting services financed by Sida is procured in competition; the rest, more than 1.6 billion SEK, is from negotiated contracts, especially with government authorities and NGOs.[8] The private and state-owned CFs in my sample accounted for 470 MSEK, that is, around 6% of Sida's total budget or 18% of Sida's total purchase of consulting services in 1998. At least 80% of this 470 MSEK is awarded in competition.[9] Foreign CFs account for 46 MSEK, which should be compared with the purchases of 903 MSEK from Swedish private CFs and individuals. The number of contracts awarded to foreign CFs is limited but increasing.

Comparisons between Sida and the Danish International Development Assistance (Danida) are shown in Table 4.3, though Danida's budget is incomplete for implementing organizations. Both of these bilateral development agencies spend around 10% to 12% of their budget on consulting services purchased from private CFs. However, a significant difference between Sida and Danida is that the 20 largest private CFs account for 468 MDKK or 73% of Danida's total purchases from private CFs on 641 MDKK, whereas the 20 largest private CFs only account for 528 MSEK or 56% of Sida's total purchases on 949 MSEK (Danida, 1998; Sida, 1999a). Thus, Sida procures more services from small CFs and individuals, which may be explained by the fact that Sida has a smaller administration and therefore needs to purchase services from them. Although not shown in the table, another difference is that Danida's purchases from other government authorities is of limited size and considerably lower than 8% of the total budget, which is Sida's proportion.[10] Finally, Danida focuses much more on purchases of goods and contractor services than Sida does.

4.3 Procurement Rules

The procurement rules differ across multilateral development agencies, as can be seen in Table 4.4 (EFCA, 1997). Basically, the development agencies focus on projects in different geographical areas. In principle, all of the listed development agencies permit only CFs from member countries to participate in the tenders.[11] The same rule applies for the staff of the CFs with the exception of

---

[8] Sida's development assistance program in Eastern Europe is heavily directed toward institutional building. Private CFs obtained 14% of the contract value in this area. State-owned CFs and government and local authorities received 26% of the contract value and NGOs received 25%. Most of the contracts with government authorities are large negotiated contracts for which private firms are not allowed to compete.

[9] According to Tables A.8 and A.9 in Appendix A, the Swedish CFs were awarded Sida contracts in competition with contract values of 256 MSEK and negotiated Sida contracts for 66 MSEK in the sample.

[10] This statement is made according to interviews with persons employed by Danida.

[11] The EU funds also permit CFs from the host countries to participate, although they are not members of the EU.

Table 4.4. Procurement rules across some multilateral development agencies.

	World Bank	AsDB	AfDB	EBRD	EU-PHARE/TACIS
Areas where projects are financed	Worldwide, both developing countries and Eastern Europe (member countries).	Asia (member countries).	Africa (member countries).	Eastern Europe (member countries).	Central Europe and Baltic countries (PHARE), former Soviet Union and Mongolia (TACIS).
Continuity of CFs from previous to succeeding stages of project	Permissable where continuity is judged to be essential. If original appointment was not based on competition, continuation normally requires competition.	Permissable where continuity is judged to be essential such as from design to project implementation.	Bank will accept proposal by borrower to retain same CF on negotiated terms. Any change of CF to be referred to bank.	Competition is preferred but continuity between phases may be allowed. Should preferably be provided for in original contract.	Generally permitted, although CFs who have designed Terms of Reference can not bid for project implementation.
Invitation or Short-listing	Usually by client, approved by bank. 3 to 6 firms from a wide geographical spread.	Loans: by client, approved by bank. TA: by bank. 5 to 7 firms showing a regional balance.	Usually by client, approved by bank. 5 to 7 firms from a wide geographical spread.	By client, approved by bank. 3 to 6 firms short-listed. Short response period (0.05-0.2 MEUR). Long response period (>0.2 MEUR).	Short-list drawn by EU. Minimum of 7 firms drawn from manifestation of interest.
CVs	Standard form. Style specified short (limits each CV to two pages). Firm representative and staff member have to sign CVs.	Style specified long (covering responsibilities in previous and proposed projects). Staff members must sign CVs.	Identical to World Bank. Staff may have to sign CVs.	No format (for EU-funded projects, EU-format).	As in tender dossier. EU requires nominated persons fulfill contract.

Table 4.4 (Continued)

	World Bank	AsDB	AfDB	EBRD	EU-PHARE/TACIS
Project summary sheets	Style not specified.	Style specified, similar to DACON sheet.	Style not specified.	As in tender dossier.	As in tender dossier/contract conditions.
Marking system	Detailed in RFP. Weighting differs across projects, but major percentage of mark is normally for personnel.	Evaluation criteria given. Personnel attract most marks, who must be available for duration of project.	Detailed in RFP. Varies across projects.	As in Invitation for Proposal.	As in tender dossier.
Selection	By competition for projects above 0.15 MUSD. Usually by client, approved by bank. TOs to be marked first with unsuitable offers rejected. FOs to be publicly opened and marked. TOs and FOs are weighted. Cost weighting normally 10% to 20% and never more than 30%.	Loans: by client, approved by bank. TA: by bank. Based on best TO only, with primary emphasis on personnel. FO then requested from the first-ranked firm.	For least complex projects based on best TO within 10% of best. FOs of "best CFs" opened and lowest accepted for negotiation. For medium complex projects, TOs and FOs are marked and weighted. In most complex projects, selection based purely on TO. FO is only considered for best marked firm.	Direct selection up to 50,000 EUR. By client, approved by bank. For larger contracts selection based on TO only. Price can be a secondary but not primary consideration.	Direct agreement for projects up to 0.05 MEUR (PHARE) and up to 0.2 MEUR (TACIS). For larger projects, client evaluation, approved by Committee (PHARE), or Committee evaluation (TACIS) of quality and price.
Negotiation	With selected firm.	With the first-ranked firm.	For the three systems above: CF with lowest cost/best marked weighted mix/best TO is called to negotiate.	With selected firm.	No, if award follows a tender. Yes, for a direct agreement.

Note: CV = curriculula vitae, DACON = data on consultants (database on CFs registered at developments banks), FO = financial offer, RFP = request for proposal, TA = technical assistance, TO = technical offer. *Source:* EFCA (1997) and own modifications.

EBRD, which permits staff from any country. Some development agencies, like the World Bank and AsDB, are more reluctant than the EU funds to let a specific CF continue from previous to succeeding steps of a project. This means that a CF that has undertaken a feasibility study is not allowed to tender for the design step. There must be at least one step in the project schedule (see also Figure 1.1) in which the CF does not participate. The motivation for this restriction is that the CF will then not be able to automatically suggest a continuation of the project, which would imply more services supplied by this CF, although the project would not be profitable to implement. The problem with the restriction, however, is that cost inefficiencies arise for the client because the CF cannot fully use scope economies. The CF has fixed costs associated with the project—for example, information and contract costs—which are now spread across a lower sales volume. When another CF steps into the project, this firm must also cover the information costs to learn what the project is about. This extra cost can be avoided if the same CF implements a larger number of services. Furthermore, the requirements and standards for curricula vitae, project summary sheets and contracts can vary greatly across development agencies (EFCA, 1997). There may also be large differences across development agencies in their focus on engineering and management services, but this topic is analyzed more closely in Chapter 7.

Since many CFs wish to tender when multilateral development agencies finance projects, these projects are announced in international papers or on the Internet, or both. Most projects require an application in which the CFs have to show interest in the project; between three and nine of them are short-listed (see also Figure 6.1). EU funds are used to invite more CFs to tender than invited by the World Bank and the regional development banks, as shown in Table 4.4. The number of short-listed firms will also increase with the size of the project. Firms that have been short-listed are then allowed to submit a proposal. Generally, the client (borrower) is allowed to short-list the CFs when the financing takes the form of loans from the World Bank or the regional development banks with the condition that the bank's tender rules are followed, whereas the banks short-list in the case of technical assistance. In EU-financed projects, on the other hand, short-lists are as a rule drawn by EU. In the final selection of the proposals, the development agencies use marking systems in which heavy weight in general is given to technical offers that also include the curricula vitae of the staff. The weight of the financial offer differs across multilateral development agencies, as can be seen in Table 4.4. As a comparison, Sida applies a selection model in which technical and financial offers are mixed and weighted at around 70% to 80% and 20% to 30%, respectively.

Clients have in recent years more to say about the short-listing and the final selection of a supplier when consulting services are procured and financed by development agencies. This freedom to the clients is under supervision by the financier so that the marking systems are followed. Practically, the consequence should be that tender evaluations of projects financed by development agencies will become similar to evaluations in the commercial market. Marketing, client visits, and social competence of the firm representatives and staff should therefore become more important elements of the strategy for the CF when operating abroad. This is especially valid for projects financed by bilateral development agencies and when the client has to finance some parts of the projects started up by multilateral development agencies. The issue of whether evaluations in projects financed by development agencies should be similar to evaluations in commercial projects is analyzed empirically in Chapter 6. Still, clients have minimal influence on the evaluation when consulting services are procured for some EU funds (e.g., EU-TACIS and EU-ALA) and for AsDB in the form of technical assistance. *An interesting observation is that the development agencies —EU funds and AsDB—that make the decision with minimal influence by the client are also the only development agencies that the CFs are allowed to visit and that seem susceptible to lobbying.*[12] In principle, it is possible for the CFs to make a person's acquaintance in the AsDB and EU administration. On the other hand, it is seldom worthwhile for the CFs to try to visit, and lobby toward, the World Bank or other regional development banks.

Most development agencies have limits above which contracts may not be awarded through direct negotiations. For example, Sida has an upper limit of 0.2 MSEK, EBRD and EU-PHARE have a limit of 50,000 EURO ($\approx$0.4 MSEK), EU-TACIS has a limit of 200,000 EURO ($\approx$1.6 MSEK) and the World Bank has a limit of 0.15 MUSD ($\approx$1.2 MSEK). A look in the database on tender documents, however, shows that Sida in particular does not follow these procurement rules for negotiated contracts. There are 34 negotiated contracts financed by Sida in the sample. Of these, 25 have a contract value above the upper limit of 0.2 MSEK, and the largest negotiated contract financed by Sida is as much as 13 MSEK. Twelve were continued negotiated contracts whose first steps may have been awarded in competition, and 13 were new negotiated contracts. Private CFs were awarded 17 contracts and state-owned CFs won 8 contracts above the limit, so these contracts were not typical negotiated contracts awarded to state-owned CFs, as discussed earlier. No negotiated contracts financed by the EU funds and EBRD are observed in the database, but the World Bank financed 9 negotiated contracts, of which 4 were above 1.2 MSEK; the largest one was a continued contract on 17 MSEK. The rest of the negotiated contracts in the database are commercial projects, where there are no restrictions.

Among the European development agencies, EBRD is clearly the most

---

[12] This observation is in accordance with key persons employed by the CFs in the sample.

commercial of the listed development agencies and assists only with loans to projects that are profitable enough so that the client will be able to pay back the loans. The EU funds PHARE, TACIS, ALA, and so on, focus only on procurement of consulting services, whereas the other development agencies have a mixed procurement of services and goods. According to interviews with key persons employed in the Swedish CFs in the sample, there are several other distinguishing characteristics of the EU funds compared with other bi- and multilateral development agencies. In contrast to the other agencies, which are seldom susceptible to lobbying, the CFs have to spend resources on marketing and lobbying toward key persons employed in the EU administration to be shortlisted. After the proposals have been submitted, the tenderers are invited to present their proposals in Brussels. The presentation may become decisive for the tender evaluation. CFs that have experience with EU funds are far from positive about them and mention several problems: complicated tendering procedures, delayed payments for completed projects and services, and a relatively low fee per hour. The EU administration has little responsibility for the projects because of the administration's lack of continuity, and administrative personnel seldom evaluate the completed projects or visit the clients. The whole procedure from invitation and tender evaluation to inspection of completed projects and payment is bureaucratic.

The fact that the development agencies have different procurement rules implies that the CF's learning of these rules can be regarded as a fixed cost that is specific for each agency. This is particularly valid when multilateral development agencies are the financiers. If a CF is only awarded a few contracts for a specific multilateral development agency, these operations will hardly be profitable. To cover the fixed costs, the CF must instead be awarded several contracts by, and have a large volume of sales for, each multilateral agency on which it focuses. It is primarily large CFs that can sell many different services to multiple projects; that is, small CFs will not be able to tender for international projects financed by multilateral development agencies in the long run. Scale in the international operations will therefore be important, in some sense, for the CFs to be profitable.

The World Bank and the regional development banks (but not the EU funds) also administer bilateral consulting funds or trust funds that are financed by each country's bilateral development agency. These funds are "earmarked," which means that only Swedish CFs can be awarded contracts financed by the Swedish trust funds. The funds cannot be used when the client is financed through loans from the World Bank or the regional development banks, but only when these banks procure for preproject purposes. Mostly, the bank's project must be approved by Sida to use resources from the trust fund. Sida may then give instructions for how the procurement among Swedish CFs and government authorities is going to be accomplished, or the banks can do this themselves. The trend is, however, that the World Bank and the regional development banks are allowed to short-list and make the procurement themselves, given that the project is approved by Sida.

4.4 Summary

The purpose of development assistance is, of course, to assist the client in the host country. First, the implemented consulting services will increase the welfare of the host country. Second, because the knowledge gap is large between CFs from developed countries and clients in emerging markets, the development agencies have to assist in preproject identifications, negotiations and postproject evaluations; otherwise the CFs may try to cheat the clients in some way. Third, the main reason that the agencies today focus more on consulting services instead of financing large turnkey projects is to facilitate knowledge transfer to emerging markets, so that clients and local firms in these markets will learn to replicate the services implemented by international CFs.

The involvement of development agencies has several consequences for the international CFs: 1) The risk that clients with low financial credibility will not pay for implemented projects is reduced for the CF, implying that competition will be stronger than in commercial projects; 2) The CFs will sell more services to emerging markets than otherwise—in fact, many of the projects would not be undertaken at all without this financing; 3) As overall sales for the CFs in emerging markets increase and become more stable, representative and even permanent offices will be established when country-specific fixed costs can be covered to a higher degree (compare with Chapter 3); and 4) Since the CFs are relatively small and sell services to many different countries, they will use the development agencies as market observers of potential projects.

When bilateral development agencies like Sida finance consulting projects, there will be fewer tenderers because the assistance is tied. These agencies will therefore function as spearheads for CFs from the same country into new markets, but they are even more important in this role when the CFs win the first contract for new clients. A drawback is that Sida procures many services directly from other government authorities, where private CFs are not even allowed to tender. This is hardly an optimal way of procurement, because no alternatives have been considered. Furthermore, Sida awards many negotiated contracts above the upper monetary limit for such contracts, including to private CFs. The procurement rules of bi- and multilateral development agencies differ from each other in several respects: whether they allow continuity from previous to succeeding steps, the number of tenderers that are short-listed, whether the client may influence the selection of supplier, and the bureaucracy involved in the tender procedures. The different tender rules can be regarded as fixed costs specific for each agency that the international CFs have to learn about, meaning that, in some sense, scale will be necessary to operate abroad.

Chapter 5

KNOWLEDGE TRANSFER

In this chapter, the analysis is focused on the development agencies as catalysts, and the consulting firms (CFs) as transferor, when knowledge and technology are transmitted to emerging markets. I discuss the elements that are necessary to include in consulting projects for the knowledge transfer to be successful, and whether the knowledge gap between developed and emerging markets is likely to increase or decrease. The role of CFs for emerging markets, and the advantages and disadvantages with turnkey projects are also examined. Finally, I empirically test how the indicators of knowledge transfer—cooperation with local firms and training—vary across the financing of the project and the development level of the host country.

5.1 Knowledge Transfer in the Consulting Sectors

Regarding procurement of consulting services, the most important role of the development agencies is perhaps that they facilitate knowledge and technology transfer from developed to emerging markets. As mentioned in Chapter 1, CFs typically collect information and knowledge that is packaged and sold as services in the form of documents and labor services. For CFs in the infrastructure sectors, knowledge includes both the technical and managerial skills necessary to supply these services. Information about technology is primarily collected from technology owners and generators in the home country of the CFs, for example, operators, contractors and investment material suppliers, but can also be acquired when executing projects.[1] Managerial skills are acquired through learning by doing as projects are conducted (see Chapter 2). When the services are executed, it is likely that some of this knowledge is transmitted from (or via) the international CF (the transferor) to the client and local CFs in the host country (the transferees). *The knowledge transfer is expected to be particularly high and intensive when consulting services are implemented, because: 1) The suppliers are highly knowledge-intensive firms; 2) Production of services often requires direct contact and cooperation between the supplier and the buyer; and 3) Consulting services can seldom be patented, meaning that*

---

[1] CFs seldom transfer patented technology, either owned by themselves or by the technology generators in the home country.

the recipients can replicate the services in their own projects. One of the purposes of the financing of consulting services by development agencies is that the transferees in the host country will learn to master the services so that they will be capable of replicating or performing them in collaboration or independently. The transfer of knowledge can, of course, also flow directly from the technology owners in the developed country to the transferees in the emerging market in the form of hardware, joint-executed construction services, blueprints and other documents.

Knowledge can either be embodied in documents (e.g., blueprints, studies, software), in physical capital (e.g., equipment, systems, materials) or in human minds (Siggel, 1986). There are, of course, various ways to transfer such knowledge to the recipient country. These methods include the following:

1) Formal instruction through training courses
2) On-the-job training
3) Cooperation with local employees when executing projects
4) Delivery of documents or computer software
5) Delivery of hardware

The first three ways involve learning processes. The latter two involve information that can be subsequently absorbed; the learning intensity is therefore lower in these cases. Since CFs do not produce, and seldom deliver, any hardware, the CFs are primarily involved in the first four transfer methods. This is valid for all kinds of CFs, not only for those operating in the infrastructure sectors. As a result of the high learning intensity, it is claimed that the transfer is much more intensive when knowledge-based firms like CFs operate in emerging markets compared with when manufacturing firms do. Most studies that analyze knowledge transfer from developed countries to emerging markets have, in fact, only focused on manufacturing firms as the transferors, and then specifically on knowledge transfer when multinational firms undertake direct investments in foreign emerging markets. In this chapter, it is argued that knowledge is likely to be transferred when *exporting* services.

Teece (1981) says that knowledge transfer is costly. The costs can either be acquisition costs (e.g., license fees), transmission costs (e.g., local adaptations) or learning costs for the transferees (e.g., training). According to a survey on technology transfer from Canadian CFs to emerging markets by Niosi et al. (1995), the lack of expertise among the transferees to absorb the technology was the largest transfer cost. This lack in human capital among the transferees had to be improved through costly training of the transferees' personnel. The quality of the local industrial infrastructure was also associated with transfer costs. Examples of other transfer costs that were estimated to be less important were differences in technical standards between the home and host countries, low productivity in the host country and administrative restrictions.

Since a large part of the knowledge is acquired through learning processes when CFs are involved, *the transmission of knowledge requires some form of cooperation between the international CF and the transferees in the host country, either by training of the transferees in the project or by (temporary) joint ventures/cooperation between the transferor and transferees*. The inclusion of training in the project is one way to specifically focus on the transmission of know-how to the host country. *Since such training, especially of local CFs, tends to make the knowledge base in the supplying CF less valuable as the knowledge gap decreases, there are no incentives for the supplying CF to include training as one element in the projects. The initiative for including training is therefore taken by the client or the development agencies.*[2]

The organization mode of the project and the distribution of tasks between international and local CFs are of crucial influence on the effectiveness of knowledge transfer. When the organization of the project is the responsibility of development agencies, the effectiveness of knowledge transfer is partially determined outside the knowledge transmitting and receiving firms. Turnkey projects, which are supplied and executed by firms originating in developed countries and where local firms are subcontracted only for unskilled tasks, have a minimum amount of knowledge transfer. This is why development agencies seldom finance turnkey projects nowadays. When firms from developed countries organize and manage the project, but to a higher degree subcontract various tasks and services to local CFs and professionals, knowledge transfer is, according to Siggel (1986), still not likely to be large, unless training is a part of the project.

Transmission of knowledge to local CFs is also likely to occur any time that international and local CFs cooperate in a temporary joint venture in the execution of projects. The participation of local CFs can either be enforced or encouraged by the financier, which is primarily a multilateral development agency, or by the client in the case of commercial projects. Also, bilateral development agencies may induce such collaboration, but they should have fewer incentives for doing so, because they may give priority to a high reflow of income to the home country for politico-economic reasons. The cooperation

---

[2] In a Canadian survey from 1990 (Niosi et al., 1995), it was concluded that the initiative for the technology transfer was taken by the international CF (transferor) in only a few cases (7%). Most transfers were instead the initiative of the client (74%) or the development agencies (19%). The year 1990 was, however, several years before the development agencies began to focus on procurement of consulting services. Today, the share of development agencies should therefore be considerably higher.

between international and local CFs will not only transfer knowledge to the host country but may also enhance development by creating a local consulting sector (Siggel, 1986). In the beginning of the 1970s, the South Korean government forbade turnkey projects implemented by foreign firms and obliged foreign contractors to cooperate with local contractors and CFs. According to Perrin (1981), this was the main reason that a local sector of CFs was created and developed. Today, South Korean CFs have developed so far that they compete in the export market with CFs from traditional developed countries.

When local CFs are in charge of the consulting part of the project, the local knowledge base is primarily updated through learning by doing. Knowledge from developed countries can then be sourced by subcontracting specific parts to international CFs. The best guarantee that knowledge and technology will be transferred to the host country happens when the international CF owns a local office in the host country. Profit motives will then ensure that the local subsidiary receives the knowledge necessary to implement the services from other parts of the firm (Siggel, 1986). However, the establishment of a permanent office seldom occurs in emerging markets because of the sector-specific demand shocks, as discussed in Chapter 3.

According to a survey by Niosi et al. (1995), more than 50% of the transferees had acquired capabilities that they were expected to have learned through knowledge transfer, and they were able to execute projects of a similar nature. However, the learning of capabilities was weak or absent for as much as 30% of the transferees. The authors conclude that the success of knowledge transfer cannot therefore be assumed. Mytelka (1985) as well as Stewart and Nihei (1987) emphasize that the transferee must have absorptive capacity for the transfer to be successful. This capacity includes general and technical education as well as social and economic infrastructure. If the transferee lacks this capacity, transferring costs will be high because local personnel have to be trained. However, when the absorptive capacity of the transferees increases, the knowledge will be transferred at a faster pace as the recipient costs diminish. Niosi et al. (1995) suggest that successful transfer requires that the transferees get the opportunity to replicate the services. This opportunity depends on whether similar projects are initiated in the local market and whether the market for such projects is growing.

Niosi et al. (1995) also conclude that the characteristics of the transferor, the transferee and the host country, as well as the organization of the project, are important for the transfer to be successful. Among the transferors, small specialized CFs that were not diversified into other sectors (e.g., construction and manufacturing) were the most successful. Joint ventures between the transferor and transferees especially increased the likelihood that the transferees were able to replicate the capabilities that they were supposed to have learned.

Transferees with higher education (a faster and higher learning capability) that were active in research and development had a higher probability of being able to assimilate the transferred knowledge. Finally, transferees in host countries with few restrictions on technology transfer were more likely to be successful.

In the infrastructure sectors, technical calculations and design services—for example, feasibility studies and preliminary and detailed design—are mostly the first services that local CFs learn to master, and operation services are the first for the clients. Supervision and project management of construction and procurement services are more complex and take longer to learn; the most difficult services to learn are management services like institutional building, training courses, and reorganization and tariff studies.

The increased volume of training and cooperation in projects with local CFs in recent years have meant that the existing knowledge base of the international CFs has become less valuable as the knowledge gap between international and local CFs has decreased. Today, it is therefore more important for the international CFs to upgrade their knowledge base at a faster pace and to stay at least one step ahead of the competitors; otherwise, the international CFs will be driven out of business in the international market by inexpensive local CFs. This is particularly important for international CFs that focus on technical calculations and design services. In recent years, many technical consulting firms (TCFs) that originate in developed countries and are heavily focused on such services have left the international market because they have not been able to upgrade their knowledge bases fast enough compared with local CFs.

Regarding the role of CFs in emerging markets, these firms, either international or local, can also link contractors and investment material suppliers in the home and host countries. The transfer of knowledge and information may deal with existing plants, machinery construction, and research and development, but may also be related to feedback of data, specifications, norms and process information (Roberts, 1972). If the client lets an independent CF—with specific (local) knowledge for the project—procure contractor services and investment materials in an investment project, the bargaining power of the client will be increased. Such a CF will possess the knowledge to discriminate between good and bad proposal alternatives. This holds no matter whether the CF is local or international.

5.2 Organization Mode and Development Level

The organization mode of the project and the distribution of tasks between international and local CFs, contractors and investment material suppliers often depend on the development level of the host country. In developed countries, the client has mostly experienced professionals in-house who know how to operate the system or plant and how to construct it and who have their own preferences about the characteristics of the plant. The client will, therefore, use a traditional mode (see Chapter 1) and lead, plan and coordinate the implementation phase independently, but order construction and consulting services, equipment and components piecemeal from different contractors, investment material suppliers and CFs. A similar alternative is to let a CF assist the client's own professionals with project management and procurement services. Such traditional investment projects are especially common when the client is a government authority or a state-owned operator, for example, a telecom or energy operator, who has their own divisions of engineers, project planners and construction workers.[3]

Investment projects in emerging markets are implemented either through turnkey or traditional mode. Clients in emerging markets seldom possess enough knowledge and technology to design the plant, procure services and goods, or lead and coordinate the implementation. The international CF will, in emerging markets, not only assist the client's own professionals (if the client has any) as in developed countries, but will replace the client. This means that the CFs can operate much more freely with fewer client-imposed restraints and can have a much more central role and a larger responsibility for procurement, logistics and planning compared with similar projects in developed countries. In a traditional mode, the CF does not take responsibility for the construction work or financing of the project, because this would imply too large a risk. Each subcontractor is instead directly responsible to the client. Responsibility for operating the completed plant/system is not taken by the CFs. Such "build-operate-transfer" contracts (BOT contracts) are signed by contractors in turnkey projects. The technological backwardness of the client will often lead to projects on a turnkey basis, where a contractor from a developed country is responsible for a whole package of design and implementation services, as well as procurement of raw materials, systems and equipment. Client intervention is held to a minimum in a turnkey project.

The rationale for ordering turnkey is partly related to the transaction cost problem.[4] It is easier and less costly for the client to let an experienced contractor organize, lead and coordinate the different steps and suppliers in the

---

[3] The operator cannot, however, employ such professionals full time, meaning that they are often hired out to other operators in the same sector—primarily to foreign operators who are not competitors.

[4] There are also incentives for the contractor to sell turnkey. The bundling of different suppliers and products in a turnkey solution means that a unique product is created by the contractor. Since demand is led by the client, who also specifies the basic characteristics of the project such as location and output capacity, turnkey is a way for the contractor to differentiate the project as an alternative to those suggested by the competitors.

implementation phase of the project than to do this itself. A client in an emerging market perhaps orders a new plant only one or a few times in a 10-year period, whereas a contractor may have replicated the tasks necessary to set up a new plant for a variety of clients in several countries every year. If the construction and coordination costs are lower (especially if a shorter time is spent) for the contractor than for the client, both participants gain from a turnkey solution.

Even if the client is able to organize the investment independently, he or she may have the advantages of a turnkey solution because the project costs may be lower and the commissioning dates may be earlier. To let experienced contractors and CFs be responsible for the project is also seen as a guarantee of reliability in an operation, which is important in host countries where management skills are scarce. In a turnkey project, the contractors and CFs will have more responsibility, meaning that they will have more incentives to perform competently. Thus, the risk for project failure will be shifted to the contractors and CFs in a turnkey project (Roberts, 1972).

However, the turnkey mode has disadvantages. First, turnkey projects are often ill-adapted for local conditions. A new technology suited for local resources and factor endowments is seldom invented by the international contractors and CFs for each new project. This would be unprofitable for the suppliers. Second, the knowledge transfer to the host country is often small, because local firms are only allowed to execute nonskilled parts of the project. If the host country has proceeded with development and has local contractors and CFs who are able to absorb knowledge from suppliers that originate in developed countries and who know how to learn from their own experiences, a turnkey contract is often an inferior mode. In a turnkey project, it is more likely that the learning-by-doing effect is almost exclusively appropriated by the suppliers from the developed countries that become more competitive in tendering for subsequent contracts in other countries (Roberts, 1972). In fact, 10 to 15 years ago, contractors and CFs from developed countries could sell their services in a turnkey project and thereafter continue to the next project and sell the same services. Sometimes they could even return to an old client and sell similar services once again.

Now I turn to the question of whether the effectiveness of knowledge transfer depends on the development level of the host country. In the least developed countries, the local consulting sector is often nonexistent and the construction and capital goods sectors are weak. The interaction between international and local CFs is then limited and the transferees have a low education level and cannot absorb the transferred knowledge. The effectiveness of knowledge transfer is therefore low. In more developed emerging markets, there generally exists a local consulting sector. Joint ventures between international and local CFs are then possible and the local personnel are to a higher degree able to assimilate the transferred knowledge. This kind of emerging market is the one to which knowledge transfer via CFs is the most effective, according to Siggel (1986). In the most developed emerging markets, the local CFs may be in charge of the engineering and management parts of the project and may subcontract specific parts to international CFs. In fact, the local CFs in such host countries (like South Korea, Brazil and India) may even export their services to the least developed countries and participate in the retransfer of knowledge and thereby compete with CFs originating in developed countries.

We then come to the question of whether the knowledge gap between the developed and emerging markets becomes narrower or wider when CFs from the former markets operate in the latter. International CFs will upgrade their knowledge base from their own experiences (learning by doing), whereas local CFs and operators will learn both from their own experiences and from being trained by international CFs. The learning from being trained will in turn depend on the educational level of the transferees' employees. Siggel (1986) suggests that the international CF will learn more than the local CF unless a training contract is included in the project. His conclusion is then that the knowledge gap can be expected to widen between developed countries and the poorest emerging markets that have almost no local consulting sector. The reason is that partici-pation of local CFs is low in projects implemented in such host countries and the educational level in the host country is also too low, so that knowledge cannot be assimilated effectively. If the firms in the host country have reached a higher level of education and knowledge, the gap is more likely to narrow, because cooperation between international and local CFs will be more frequent and the transferees will be more able to absorb knowledge through training courses. Thus, the gap between the most and the least developed emerging markets should increase.

5.3 Transfer through Training and Cooperation

Here, I will empirically analyze how the two indicators of knowledge transfer—training and cooperation with local firms—are related to different financing groups and development levels of the host countries. Table 5.1 depicts how often training is included in the projects across financing alternatives in our sample. To make the commercial group of projects comparable with the three development agency groups, I have chosen to exclude 39 tender documents submitted to developed markets. The statistics indicate that it is primarily the development agencies, and not the clients, that are the main initiators of training of personnel employed by the clients and local CFs in the host country. Sida and

Table 5.1. Training included in projects in emerging markets across financing groups for all tenders and negotiations in number and percent.

Financing group	Training included in						Pure training projects	
	all projects		investment projects		restructuring projects			
	Number	%	Number	%	Number	%	Number	%
Sida	43 (162)	27	21 (97)	22	22 (65)	34	11	7
EU funds	12 (46)	26	4 (21)	19	8 (25)	32	1	2
Other MDAs	15 (105)	14	6 (61)	10	9 (44)	20	1	1
Commercial	12 (106)	11	4 (75)	5	8 (31)	26	6	6
Total	82 (419)	20	35 (254)	14	47 (165)	28	19	5

Note: Total number of tender documents in parentheses. All projects in developed countries have been excluded to make the commercial group comparable with the other groups. None of the projects in developed countries included any training. MDAs = multilateral development agencies.

the EU funds, in particular, often include training as a component in the projects. Training seems to be more frequent in restructuring projects than in investment projects, partly depending on pure training projects belonging to the former group.

The inclusion of training in the project can be seen as a measure of a high intensity of knowledge transfer, but it can also reflect the transferees' capability of absorbing that knowledge is low and that this capability must be improved by training programs (Siggel, 1986; Stewart and Nihei, 1987). These indications do not exclude each other but can be true at the same time. If the latter hypothesis is true, then one would expect that the lower the competence and education level among the transferees, the higher the probability of including training. In Table 5.2, we compare the development level of the host country with the inclusion of training in the project. Since no measure of the transferees' absorption capacity or education level are available, we have to use GDP per capita as a proxy for the host country's absorptive capacity. The pattern in the table is not unambiguous, but, in general, projects undertaken in host countries with a low GDP per capita have a higher probability of including some form of training. This is in line with the hypothesis by Siggel (1986) and Stewart and Nihei (1987), as stated earlier, that training is necessary in host countries with low absorptive capacity to make knowledge and technology transfer possible.

To measure the strength of the linear relationship between inclusion of training in the project and GDP per capita of the host country, I estimate a Pearson correlation coefficient between these two factors. The estimate is -0.12,

Table 5.2. Training included in projects across development level of the host country for all tenders and negotiations in number and percent.

GDP per capita 1996	Training included in						Pure training projects	
	all projects		investment projects		restructuring projects			
	Number	%	Number	%	Number	%	Number	%
< $2,000	33 (139)	24	17 (84)	20	16 (55)	29	7	5
$2,000-$4,000	19 (92)	21	7 (62)	11	12 (30)	40	2	2
$4,000-$6,000	13 (77)	17	2 (48)	4	11 (29)	38	4	5
$6,000-$8,000	12 (53)	23	5 (28)	18	7 (25)	28	5	10
> $8,000	3 (62)	5	1 (46)	2	2 (16)	13	1	2
Total	80 (423)	19	32 (268)	12	48 (155)	31	19	4

Note: GDP per capita is PPP adjusted and taken from WDI (1997). There are 35 missing observations for countries which have no measurable GDP per capita (e.g., Bosnia, Palestine, Somalia). Total number of tender documents in parentheses.

significant with a 95% confidence level.[5] Thus, a high development level seems to be related to a low probability that training is included in the project, and vice versa.

Now we turn to the other measure of knowledge transfer: cooperation or joint ventures with local CFs. We expect that joint ventures between international and local CFs would be most frequent for projects financed by multilateral development agencies or the client (commercial), because bilateral development agencies would have incentives to give priority to a high reflow of incomes to the donor country. In the upper part of Table 5.3, surprisingly, joint ventures are least frequent in commercial projects—in only 33% of them—at the same time as 52% to 64% of the projects that are financed by multilateral development agencies and Sida include a joint venture or cooperation between the tenderer and local CFs. However, we neither take into account the amount of services that are implemented by the local CF in each project nor how large each project is in contract value. In the lower part of Table 5.3, the average planned time spent by local CFs (weighted with project value) is described for

---

[5] The coefficient can take on any value between -1 and 1. An estimate of 1 means a perfect positive linear relationship, 0 means no linear relationship at all, and -1 means a perfect negative linear relationship between the two variables. A 95% confidence level implies that there is only a 5% probability that I will reject a true hypothesis that there is no relationship at all between the two variables in the population. The number of observations equals 423 in this correlation estimation.

Table 5.3. Joint ventures with local CFs in projects in emerging markets across financing groups for all tenders and negotiations in number and percent.

| Financing group | Number of joint ventures with local CFs in | | | | | |
| | all projects | | investment projects | | restructuring projects | |
	Number	%	Number	%	Number	%
Sida	86 (162)	53	63 (97)	65	23 (65)	35
EU funds	24 (46)	52	11 (21)	52	13 (25)	52
Other MDAs	67 (105)	64	44 (61)	72	23 (44)	52
Commercial	35 (106)	33	28 (75)	37	7 (31)	23
Total	212 (419)	51	146 (254)	57	66 (165)	40

| Financing group | Local CFs' planned share (time spent) in | | |
| | all projects | investment projects | restructuring projects |
	%	%	%
Sida	16	20	10
EU funds	13	9	18
Other MDAs	27	31	20
Commercial	28	31	7
Total	23	26	14

Note: Total number of tender documents in parentheses. All projects in developed countries have been excluded in order to make the commercial group comparable with the other groups. MDAs = multilateral development agencies.

projects across financing groups. Commercial projects and projects financed by other multilateral development agencies clearly have a higher local content than do Sida and EU projects. Furthermore, local cooperation is more frequent in investment projects than in restructuring projects. This may partly depend on local CFs being more skilled in technology than in management and partly on investment projects perhaps needing more local knowledge about local conditions and environments.

From the previous discussion, one could say that the higher the development level of the host country, the more frequent the joint ventures between international and local CFs are expected to be. In the least developed host countries, there are simply seldom any local CFs with which to cooperate. In the upper part of Table 5.4, however, the probability is the highest that joint ventures occur in projects in middle-income emerging markets. For the $4,000 to $6,000 and

Table 5.4. Joint ventures with local CFs in projects across development level of the host country for all tenders and negotiations in number and percent.

GDP per capita 1996	Number of joint ventures with local CFs in					
	all projects		investment projects		restructuring projects	
	Number	%	Number	%	Number	%
< $2,000	61 (139)	44	42 (84)	50	19 (55)	35
$2,000-$4,000	56 (92)	61	39 (62)	63	17 (30)	57
$4,000-$6,000	47 (77)	61	33 (48)	69	14 (29)	48
$6,000-$8,000	23 (53)	43	16 (28)	57	7 (25)	28
> $8,000	27 (62)	44	21 (46)	46	6 (16)	38
Total	214 (423)	51	151 (268)	56	63 (155)	41

GDP per capita 1996	Local CFs' planned share (time spent) in		
	all projects	investment projects	restructuring projects
	%	%	%
< $2,000	21	22	16
$2,000-$4,000	18	22	10
$4,000-$6,000	18	21	14
$6,000-$8,000	30	35	9
> $8,000	27	29	18
Total	23	26	14

Note: GDP per capita is PPP adjusted and taken from WDI (1997). There are 35 missing observations for countries which have no measurable GDP per capita (e.g., Bosnia, Palestine, Somalia). Total number of tender documents in parentheses.

$6,000 to $8,000 income groups, there were planned joint ventures between the tenderer and local CFs in 61% of the projects. When considering how much time spent was planned for local CFs in the projects in the lower part of Table 5.4, on the other hand, the pattern becomes different.[6] The higher the development level of the host country, the higher the share that local CFs get. As much as 27% to 30% of the services in the projects were planned to be executed by local CFs in the two highest income groups, whereas only around 20% of the services in

---

[6] The planned share of time spent by local CFs in the lower part of Table 5.3 has been estimated for each project. An average has then been calculated for all projects in a group where each project is weighted with the project's contract value.

projects were planned for local CFs in the middle- and low-income markets.

5.4 Summary

The main reason that development agencies today focus more on consulting services than on financing large turnkey projects is to facilitate knowledge transfer to emerging markets, so that clients and local firms in these markets will learn to replicate the services executed by international CFs. There are strong arguments for such transfers being particularly high and intensive in consulting sectors: 1) CFs are highly knowledge intensive; 2) Production of the services often requires close cooperation between the CF and the client; and 3) Services can seldom be patented, meaning that local CFs can freely replicate the services in their own projects.

Training of, and cooperation with, the client or local firms are necessary elements in the project to make the knowledge transfer effective. Since the transfer will make the knowledge base of the international CFs less valuable, these CFs have no incentives to train, or to transfer know-how to, local firms. This transfer must instead be induced by the client or the development agencies. The international CFs have then to continuously upgrade their knowledge bases if they wish to be competitive in the international market. The transferees, on the other hand, must have some capacity to assimilate the knowledge. This capacity can be improved through costly training. In fact, the empirical analysis shows that it is the development agencies, rather than the clients, that include training in the projects. Furthermore, the lower the development level of the host country, the more likely training is to be included in the project, whereas cooperation with local CFs occurs more frequently with a higher development level of the host country. In the least developed countries, there are seldom any local CFs with which to cooperate. Since the poorest countries have a low ability to learn, it is expected that the knowledge gap between the least and most developed emerging markets will increase as consulting projects are implemented. The latter countries may even catch up to the developed countries.

Chapter 6

SUCCESS FACTORS WHEN TENDERING

In this chapter, I empirically analyze which competitive factors and strategies are successful when consulting firms (CFs) tender for new assignments abroad, which is one of the main issues of the book. First, alternative tender systems are presented. Thereafter, the factors that influence the invitation of firms to participate in the tender are analyzed. Also examined is the affect of different strategies and competitive factors by the tenderers on the probability of being awarded the contract when they submit a detailed tender document or proposal. Finally, negotiated contracts are analyzed. The analysis and conclusions in this chapter are valid for all kind of CFs, irrespective of the sectors in which they operate.

6.1 Alternative Tender Systems

Consulting services can be purchased either with or without competition. In the latter case, the financier/client invites a CF for direct negotiation. In competition, however, there are three main relevant tender systems for procurement of consulting services, which are shown in Figure 6.1. These tender systems can either involve: 1) one competitive step for the firm, where the firm chooses directly whether to submit a proposal (Model I); or 2) two sequential competitive steps where the first step involves an invitation or prequalification. Thereafter, the invited firms submit proposals for final selection in the second step. The invitation may be undertaken without (Models II) or with (Model III) application for participation. In all three models, the financier/client makes the final selection among the firms that have submitted proposals.

The choice of tender system is different across financing groups. Model I, the least frequently used tender system, is rarely used outside of architecture competitions. Model II is applied for most commercial tenders in competition. The same tender system is used when Sida and its corresponding bilateral development agencies in other countries procure consulting services. Model III, where the CFs must apply for participation, is sometimes used in commercial projects and almost always when multilateral development agencies procure consulting services in competition. Multilateral development agencies have a prequalification step (Model III) for good reason: too many CFs would otherwise submit proposals because the financing of the project is guaranteed.

Figure 6.1. Alternative tender systems.

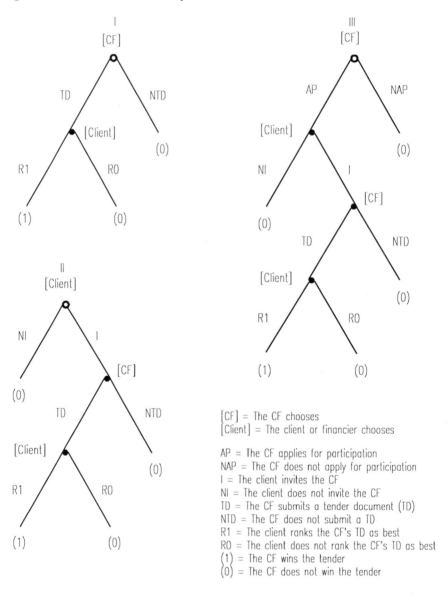

[CF] = The CF chooses
[Client] = The client or financier chooses

AP = The CF applies for participation
NAP = The CF does not apply for participation
I = The client invites the CF
NI = The client does not invite the CF
TD = The CF submits a tender document (TD)
NTD = The CF does not submit a TD
R1 = The client ranks the CF's TD as best
R0 = The client does not rank the CF's TD as best
(1) = The CF wins the tender
(0) = The CF does not win the tender

When the CFs are invited to participate in the tender, either with (Model III) or without (Model II) application for participation, they have neither submitted a detailed proposal, nor visited the client. For the invitation, the experience and skills of the whole firm are, therefore, expected to be the most important competitive factors. When development agencies assist with the financing of the project, they are often, together with the client, responsible for the invitation and final selection of the CFs.[1]

In the second last node of either Model I, II or III, the CF chooses whether to submit a tender document or not. This document consists of detailed information about the firm's experience and previous assignments, the skills and experience of the firm's team leader and other employees who will work on the project, and the price level and technical and organizational offers about how to implement the tasks in the project. In connection with the tender document, the CF will also undertake different strategic actions, such as visits to the client and cooperation with other firms. After that, the financier/client will make the final decision about which CF to select. The tender in these models can be regarded as a sealed bid for the participating firms. The tenderers do not know what the competitors' tender documents include. Although the tenderers are not always able to identify the competitors, they do have an idea about *how many* competitors will submit proposals. Whether the tenderer can identify the competitors depends on whether the financier of the project gives this information to the tenderers or not. Here, the development agencies have different policies.

6.2 Competition Step 1: Prequalification and Invitation

In this section, the first step of competition for international contracts is empirically analyzed, that is, which factors determine why a CF is invited to participate in the tender. First, I have to select a subsample of proposals from the whole sample of proposals (see Appendix A for a full description of the database). If the CF is a subconsultant to another firm—either a contractor or another CF—the latter firm will be invited, will specify the tender document and will undertake the necessary strategies to win the assignment. Since the competitive factors of the subconsultant are then less relevant and this firm will be passive, such observations are therefore omitted in the analysis of both the first and second step of competition.[2] These criteria imply that about 10% of the 358 proposals submitted in competition are excluded and that a sample of 316 observations remains in the empirical analysis; that is, there are 316 observations where the firm has been invited *and* decided to submit a proposal. The number of invitations corresponding to this sample is, in fact, larger than 316, because the firms sometimes decide not to participate even though they are invited. According to the firms in the sample, they participate in 85% to 90% of all cases when they are invited or short-listed. This high percentage is partly

---

[1] For a more detailed information about whether the client is allowed to influence the selection of supplier and differences in other tender procedures across development agencies, see Table 5.4.

[2] Of course, all negotiated contracts are excluded.

explained by the fact that when the projects are financed by multilateral development agencies, the CF has already decided to participate when it applies for participation. In principle, the CF has then committed itself to the financier to submit a proposal if it is short-listed.[3] Furthermore, 100% of the 316 proposals in the sample belong either to Models II or III, implying that all observations are associated with some form of invitation or short-listing and Model I is not applied in this chapter.

When analyzing factors that influence the invitation, one would preferably have information on tenders in which the firms have been invited, and on those in which they have not been invited. The second group of observations is, of course, almost impossible to collect and is not available in the database. Therefore I have to use another method. First, I calculate averages for relevant factors in the sample of 316 observations, which should affect the probability that the firm is invited. These figures are then compared with averages for the same factors in the 100 most important foreign markets where the same tenderers operate. Here, each firm has a weight corresponding to how many times it is included in the sample.[4] As suggested in the previous section, firm-specific characteristics should, primarily, influence the invitation, because no detailed tender document with technical and organizational solutions and staff intended to be used in the project has been specified. In Table 6.1, various factors that should affect the invitation are shown. These factors include the tenderer's previous experience with the host country and the client, whether the tenderer has a local office (permanent or representative) in the host country, and how many similar assignments the tenderer has had abroad. As discussed in Chapter 2, these explanatory factors are related to: 1) the adverse selection problem (asymmetric information), that is, signals about the tenderer's competence and experience; and 2) the need for good communication and cooperation between the CF and the client, that is, long-term relationship factors.

In general, the tenderer had previous experience with the host country and the client, and had a local office in the host country in 73%, 35% and 21%, respectively, of all tenders. These percentages should be compared to the last row, where we have calculated averages for the firms' experiences in the 100 most important foreign markets.[5] These averages are 43%, 5% to 10% and 6%,

---

[3] Refraining from submitting a proposal occurs sometimes when Sida finances the projects or when the projects are commercial.

[4] A firm that has 47 tender documents in the sample has a weight of 0.15 (47/316) when calculating averages for the 100 markets.

[5] The tenderers' experience of similar assignments in the 100 markets cannot be evaluated. The firms had a local office in 6% of the markets, which is a very high figure. This is explained by the fact that the five largest exporters, Swedtel, SwedPower, Hifab, SWECO and ÅF, have a large weight in the sample, with 5 to 18 foreign offices each (see Table 3.3).

Table 6.1. Factors that may influence the invitation of CFs (number and percent).

| Financing groups | Number of proposals | Percent of observations in the sample where the tenderers have | | | Average number of similar assignments abroad for the tenderers |
		Host country experience	Client experience	Local office	
Sida	106	69%	24%	18%	9.6
EU funds	45	60%	18%	9%	6.5
Other MDAs	87	74%	37%	23%	11.5
Commercial	78	86%	60%	28%	14.7
Total sample	316	73%	35%	21%	10.9

| | Percent of the 100 most important foreign markets where the CFs have | | |
	Host country experience	Client experience	Local office
Weighted means for 100 foreign markets	43%	5-10%	6%

Note: MDAs = multilateral development agencies. The last row should be interpreted in the following way. On average, the CFs included in the sample have previous experience with the market in 43 of the 100 most important foreign markets. In 5% to 10% of the cases, the firms have previous experience with the potential clients in these 100 markets, and in 6 of these 100 markets the firms have established a local office. When calculating these means, each CF in the sample has got a weight corresponding to how many times it is included in the sample.

respectively, that is, considerably lower for all three variables. The result indicates that these three firm-specific factors are important determinants for the invitation. *Thus, some form of minimum competence or experience of the CF is required in order to be invited.* It may also be that the CF gives priority to tenders where it has good values of the aforementioned experience factors. A representative office is, for example, a fixed cost in the host country for the CF, meaning that the firm must have a large sales volume in that specific country over which to spread these fixed costs. Therefore, the CF will focus on such host countries. Another look in the database shows that firms that have a long history of exporting are often the firms that are invited to participate in tenders.

It becomes even more interesting when comparing different financing groups. Here, the sample of projects is divided into four financing groups with relatively homogenous tender rules and competitive structures within each group: 1) Sida projects; 2) projects financed by EU funds; 3) projects financed by other multilateral development agencies (World Bank, regional development

banks, UN); and 4) commercial projects.[6] There are a limited number of
Swedish CFs operating abroad in each sector. For that reason, such firms will
almost always be invited by Sida if the sector of the project corresponds to the
firms' sector of operation. The averages for projects financed by Sida are therefore uninteresting for this specific issue. For the other three financing groups,
the averages of all four firm-specific factors are the highest for commercial
projects and the lowest for projects financed by EU funds. In the case of
previous contracts for the client, the figure is as high as 60% for commercial
projects. One explanation for this pattern is that the client is responsible for the
invitation in commercial projects. In projects financed by other multilateral
development agencies, the client is usually responsible for the short-listing of
the interested CFs, though this must be approved by the financier, and in EU
projects, a committee chosen by the EU is responsible for the short-listing. *The
more influence that the client has on the invitation, the more important are the
firm-specific factors.*

6.3 Competition Step 2: Tender Document and Final Selection

6.3.1 Hypotheses

As was shown in Figure 6.1, each tenderer submits a proposal before the finan-
cier/client makes the final selection. In this section, I empirically examine which
factors determine the outcome of the tender evaluation among the firms that
have submitted tender documents, that is, the second step of competition. Here,
too, I have 316 observations.[7] In contrast to commercial projects, most development agencies have strict rules for procurement of consulting services. When
the proposals are evaluated, these agencies use point systems where common

---

[6] The five projects in the sample financed by Nordic development agencies are included in the
Sida group. The reason for their inclusion is that when the Nordic development agencies finance
the projects, the tender rules are similar to those of Sida and the competition among the CFs is
limited to those firms originating in the few member countries.

[7] An objection against the sample could be that the firm has been invited to tender rather than
having chosen to tender, as was shown in Figure 6.1. This will, however, not cause sample
selection bias or other problems, because an invitation is determined by other factors and takes
place in an earlier stage, before the proposals are submitted and evaluated. Thus, the decisions
about which firms to invite and which firm to award the assignment to are obviously sequential.
Here, I am only interested in the last step where the client or financier definitely selects a firm,
irrespective of whether it is Model I, II or III. However, because the type of model (tender system)
partly will determine the number of competitors, it is necessary to control for the competition level
in the analysis. Finally, I assume, in line with Models I-III, that the firm only submits a proposal
if it expects to have a chance to win the contract.

weights are given to different factors as follows: 1) The competence and experience of the staff who will implement the tasks in the project and the composition of the team get a weight of at least 40%. A curriculum vitae is important, especially for the merits of the team leader; 2) The technical and organizational offers and the methodology are given a weight of around 20%; 3) The general experience of the tendering firm has a weight of around 20%; and 4) The price offer gets a weight of 15% to 25% (EFCA, 1997).

A problem is, however, that the evaluation of experience and competence is likely to be subjective; that is, it is possible to manipulate the points awarded for specific factors in the evaluation—either consciously or unconsciously. Not surprisingly, many CFs operating abroad also use other competitive factors and strategies when tendering, such as: 1) long-term relationships with the clients wherein previous clients are prioritized and the tenderer visits the client before the tender document is submitted; and 2) local networks that establish offices in the host country and cooperate with local CFs and engineers.[8] What is interesting here is that such long-term relationships and local network factors are awarded zero points in the evaluations done by the development agencies. Today, we do not know how large an influence such factors have for the outcome of the tender evaluation. If these factors do have a significant impact on the outcome, then a practical policy implication would be either to skip, or at least to relax, the strict rules for procurement applied by the development agencies, or to strengthen the sanctions associated with violations of the rules.

According to the theoretical reasoning in Chapter 2, repeat purchases and long-term relationship factors are essential when it is difficult to evaluate the quality of the services a priori and when communication and cooperation—which also are difficult to evaluate a priori—are necessary between the supplier and client. One way to develop or improve such long-term relationships is to visit the client. When it is difficult to evaluate the services a priori, also, the competence and experience of the tendering firm and its staff are then "signals" to the client/financier about the firm's ability to implement the project and should be important for the outcome. Clients have more to say in recent years about the selection of a supplier when development agencies procure consulting services, and so this kind of procurement should become more similar to procurement in the commercial market where repeat purchases are frequent. Thus, one can expect that long-term relationship factors should also become more important for projects financed by development agencies. The group of commercial projects where there are no restrictions for procurement will be a reference

---

[8] With long-term relationships I mean confidence bonds and "networks" between the CF and the client, whereas local networks mean networks with local CFs, decision makers and knowledge about the host country market.

group when testing which factors affect the choice of CF across financing alternatives. Local offices are hypothesized to have a positive influence on the probability of winning the tender because they can be used to get information about potential projects and to create networks with local CFs, decision makers and potential clients. If the local office is permanent, transportation costs can be saved by subcontracting services to it and if it is located in an emerging market, labor costs can also be saved. A minority ownership in a local CF should be enough to increase the CF's credibility as a long-term cooperator with the local CF.

To test how different factors influence the outcome of the evaluation, it must be possible to measure these factors across all proposals. Many times, the financier or client requires specific experiences of the tenderer and its staff, for example, at least three years of work in Poland or five years of experience in project management for district heating plants. Obviously, such factors cannot be measured across all proposals. Other factors that are important in almost all tenders, for example, the composition of the team or how well the proposal is designed and composed, cannot be measured in a satisfying way. Instead, I must concentrate on identifying the general experience and competence factors of the tendering firm and its staff that can easily be measured across all kinds of tender documents. Examples of measurable factors that I have included in the question-naire (see Appendix B) are the education level and international experience (years) of the tenderer's team leader, whether the tenderer had previous experience with the host country or not, and previous contracts for the client or not.

The explanatory factors that are examined and tested can be divided into five groups, as can be seen in Table 6.2. In this table, the means of the variables for won and lost tenders as well as the expected impact on the probability of winning the tender are shown. The first group of factors is related to the tendering firm's experience and the second group to the team leader's education and international experience. The third group reflects long-term relationship factors, the fourth group local network and local presence factors and the final group represents miscellaneous factors that I want to control for. Although communication and cooperation between the CF and the client is expected to be a crucial factor, it is not expected that the CF's ability to use the same language as the client will have any impact on the final selection. If the CF and the client cannot speak the same language (for example, English), then the CF will not be invited or, alternatively, will choose not to submit a proposal. Thus, the language factor will rather be decisive for the first invitation step.

Table 6.2. Basic statistics and hypotheses for the explanatory variables.

Description of explanatory variables		Means			Expected impact on the probability to win the tender
		All	Won	Lost	
Tendering firm's experience	Experience abroad with similar projects (number)	10.94	11.87	10.41	+
	Experience with the host country (dummy)	0.73	0.77	0.71	+
	Experience with the financier (dummy)	0.64	0.63	0.65	+
Characteristics of the team leader	Team leader's degree of education (years)	6.23	6.50	6.07	+
	Team leader's international experience (years)	9.34	10.09	8.91	+
LTR factors	Tenderer's experience with the client (dummy)	0.35	0.44	0.30	+
	Tenderer visited the client (dummy)	0.69	0.75	0.66	+
Local network factors	Local office in the host country (dummy)	0.21	0.28	0.16	+
	Cooperation with local CFs (percent)	13.92	12.13	14.95	+
Other factors	Size of the assignment (million SEK)	7.70	4.92	9.29	-
	Cooperation with international CFs (dummy)	0.49	0.42	0.53	?
	Distance between Sweden and the host country (kilometers)	1,803	2,197	1,578	-
Number of observations		316	115	201	xxx

Note: LTR = long-term relationship. Dummy means that the variable either takes on the value of 1 or 0. For example, if the firm has previous experience with the host country, this variable equals 1, and if the firm has no experience with the host country, the variable equals 0. A '+' means that a high value of the explanatory variable has a positive expected impact on the probability to win the tender, a '-' means that a high value has a negative expected impact, and a '?' that the impact is unsettled.

6.3.2 Bivariate Analysis

Since I consider only a *sample* of tender documents, I have to apply statistical tests in order to make conclusions about the whole *population* of tender documents. One relevant hypothesis to test is whether there is a significant difference in the success ratio across strategic alternatives; for example, one could test how the success ratio relates to whether the tenderer visited the client or not, or whether the team leader had a secondary school, university or post-university education. When considering cross-tabulations for an explanatory variable and the outcome of the tender evaluation (as can be seen in Tables 6.3 to 6.8), a chi-square test is a relevant statistical test. The higher the value of this chi-square test, the higher is the probability that there is a difference in the success ratio across strategic alternatives in the population. One usually claims

Table 6.3. The tenderer's previous experience with the host country related to awarded and lost tenders (number and percent).

The CF has previous experience with the host country		Number of tenders				Chi-square tests
		Won	Lost	All	%Won	
No		26	59	85	31	
Yes		89	142	231	39	1.69
Total		115	201	316	36	
Sida	No	13	20	33	39	
	Yes	33	40	73	45	0.31
	Total	46	60	106	43	
EU funds	No	3	15	18	17	Too few observations in cells
	Yes	7	20	27	26	
	Total	10	35	45	22	
Other multilateral DAs	No	8	15	23	35	
	Yes	20	44	64	31	0.10
	Total	28	59	87	32	
Commercial	No	2	9	11	18	Too few observations in cells
	Yes	29	38	67	43	
	Total	31	47	78	40	

Note: None of the chi-square tests is significant. The cutoff points for this test are 6.63, 3.84 and 2.71 for one degree of freedom at the 1, 5 and 10% significance level, respectively. DAs = development agencies.

Table 6.4. The team leader's degree of education related to awarded and lost tenders (number and percent).

The team leader's degree of education		Number of tenders				Chi-square tests
		Won	Lost	All	%Won	
Secondary school (S)		16	32	48	33	
University (U)		79	149	228	35	3.86
Postuniversity (PU)		20	20	40	50	
Total		115	201	316	36	
Sida	S	7	11	18	39	
	U	31	40	71	44	0.24
	PU	8	9	17	47	
	Total	46	60	106	43	
EU funds	S	0	1	1	0	Too few
	U	9	28	37	24	observations in
	PU	1	6	7	14	cells
	Total	10	35	45	22	
Other multilateral DAs	S	5	8	13	38	
	U	15	47	62	24	8.59 **
	PU	8	4	12	67	
	Total	28	59	87	32	
Commercial	S	4	12	16	25	Too few
	U	24	34	58	41	observations in
	PU	3	1	4	75	cells
	Total	31	47	78	40	

Note: ***, ** and * indicate that the chi-square test is significant at the 1%, 5% and 10% significance level, respectively. The corresponding cutoff points for this test are 9.21, 5.99 and 4.61 for two degrees of freedom. DAs = development agencies.

that the relationship must be statistically significant with at least 95% confidence to be sure that there is a relationship at all.[9] When the significance level is between 90% and 95%, the relationship is considered to be in a grey zone, where there *probably* is a relationship.

For the tenderer's experience with the host country in Table 6.3, the tende-

---

[9] The probability is then only 5% that one will reject a true null hypotheses, where the null hypothesis is that there is no relationship at all.

Table 6.5. The team leader's international experience related to awarded and lost tenders (number and percent)..

The team leader's international experience		Number of tenders				Chi-square tests
		Won	Lost	All	%Won	
0-5 years		30	69	99	30	
5-10 years		27	49	76	36	2.98
10-15 years		58	83	141	41	
Total		115	201	316	36	
Sida	0-5	10	27	37	27	
	5-10	12	16	28	43	7.87 **
	10-15	24	17	41	59	
	Total	46	60	106	43	
EU funds	0-5	4	9	13	31	Too few
	5-10	3	9	12	25	observations in
	10-15	3	17	20	15	cells
	Total	10	35	45	22	
Other multilateral DAs	0-5	4	12	16	25	
	5-10	8	14	22	36	0.56
	10-15	16	33	49	33	
	Total	28	57	87	32	
Commercial	0-5	12	21	33	36	
	5-10	4	10	14	29	1.85
	10-15	15	16	31	48	
	Total	31	47	78	40	

Note: ***, ** and * indicate that the chi-square test is significant at the 1%, 5% and 10% significance level, respectively. The corresponding cutoff points for this test are 9.21, 5.99 and 4.61 for two degrees of freedom. DAs = development agencies.

rer's success ratios are 39% and 31%, respectively, when the CF has experience, and has no experience with the host country. This difference is not significant according to the chi-square test. Thus, one cannot reject the hypothesis that there is no relationship in the population between previous experience with the host country and the probability of winning the contract in the final selection. The same conclusion is reached for the projects financed by Sida and multilateral development agencies. The chi-square test requires that there are at least five observations in each cell, and so I will not calculate any test statistics for finan-

Table 6.6. The tenderer's experience with the client related to awarded and lost tenders (number and percent).

The CF has previous experience of the client		Number of tenders				Chi-square tests
		Won	Lost	All	%Won	
No		64	140	204	31	
Yes		51	61	112	46	6.27 **
Total		115	201	316	36	
Sida	No	31	50	81	38	
	Yes	15	10	25	60	3.67 *
	Total	46	60	106	43	
EU funds	No	6	31	37	16	Too few
	Yes	4	4	8	50	observations in
	Total	10	35	45	22	cells
Other multilateral DAs	No	19	36	55	35	
	Yes	9	23	32	28	0.38
	Total	28	59	87	32	
Commercial	No	8	23	31	26	
	Yes	23	24	47	49	4.17 **
	Total	31	47	78	40	

Note: ***, ** and * indicate that the chi-square test is significant at the 1%, 5% and 10% significance level, respectively. The corresponding cutoff points for this test are 6.63, 3.84 and 2.71 for one degree of freedom. DAs = development agencies.

cing groups where this requirement is not fulfilled. In Table, 6.3, this is the case for the projects financed by EU funds and for commercial projects, although these groups indicate a much higher success ratio for proposals submitted in host countries with which the tenderer had experience.

In Tables 6.4 and 6.5, similar cross-tabulations are shown between the team leader's degree of education and international experience on the one hand, and awarded and lost tenders on the other. At a first glance, a higher education seems to be positively related to a high success ratio, for all observations and for the other multilateral and commercial groups. However, the overall group fails to show any significant chi-square test; the test for the multilateral group is significant but the interpretation is ambiguous because the success ratio is lowest for university level; and the commercial group is not testable. Sida does not take much account of the team leader's degree of education, which is also

Table 6.7. The tenderer's visits to the clients related to awarded and lost tenders (number and percent).

The CF visited the client		Number of tenders				Chi-square tests
		Won	Lost	All	%Won	
No		29	69	98	30	
Yes		86	132	218	39	2.84 *
Total		115	201	316	36	
Sida	No	9	29	38	24	
	Yes	37	31	68	54	9.37 ***
	Total	46	60	106	43	
EU funds	No	3	12	15	20	Too few
	Yes	7	23	30	23	observations in
	Total	10	35	45	22	cells
Other	No	12	10	22	55	
multilateral DAs	Yes	16	49	65	25	6.75 ***
	Total	28	59	87	32	
Commercial	No	5	18	23	22	
	Yes	26	29	55	47	4.42 **
	Total	31	47	78	40	

Note: ***, ** and * indicate that the chi-square test is significant at the 1%, 5% and 10% significance level, respectively. The corresponding cutoff points for this test are 6.63, 3.84 and 2.71 for one degree of freedom. DAs = development agencies.

supported when one takes a closer look at the different tender evaluation systems that this agency applies (Sida, 1999b). When one studies the international experience of the team leader, the opposite result is found. Here, Sida seems to take the experience of the team leader into account. For projects financed in other ways, the experience of the team leader has no significant relation to the success ratio.

In Table 6.6, cross-tabulations are described between whether the tenderer had previous contracts for the client and awarded and lost tenders. For all financing groups except other multilateral development agencies, previous experience of the client seems to increase the probability that the tenderer wins the contract. Thus, repeat purchases seem to be frequent in the consulting sectors, even though the projects are purchased in competition. Similar cross-tabulations and chi-square tests for the tenderer's visits to the client are analyzed in Table 6.7.

Table 6.8. The tenderer's local offices related to awarded and lost tenders (number and percent).

The CF has a local office in the host country		Number of tenders				Chi-square tests
		Won	Lost	All	%Won	
Permanent office	No	103	193	296	35	5.14 **
	Yes	12	8	20	60	
Representative office	No	95	176	271	35	1.47
	Yes	20	25	45	44	
Permanent or representative office	No	83	168	251	33	
	Yes	32	33	65	49	5.83 **
	Total	115	201	316	36	

Note: ***, ** and * indicate that the chi-square test is significant at the 1%, 5% and 10% significance level, respectively. The corresponding cutoff points for this test are 6.63, 3.84 and 2.71 for one degree of freedom.

There is a strong positive relationship between visits and success ratio for Sida-financed and commercial projects. No test can be done for the EU group because there are too few observations in one of the cells. Even more confusing is the fact that visits to the client seem to have a strong negative relationship with the success ratio when other multilateral development agencies are involved. I have not, however, taken into account whether the client is allowed to influence the tender evaluation.

There are only a few cases where the tenderer has a permanent office in the host country and submits an export proposal to that country. As shown in Table 6.8, the success ratio is as high as 60% compared to 35% in host countries where no permanent office is established—a statistically significant difference. Although tender documents that are submitted to host countries where the tenderer has a representative office have a slightly higher success ratio than where the tenderer has no such office, this difference is not significant.

6.3.3 Multivariate Analysis

The limitation with cross-tabulations and chi-square tests between a *single* explanatory variable and the outcome of the tender evaluation is that there are other factors that influence the outcome that I do not control for. I also wish to control for whether the client is allowed to influence the selection when the project is financed by development agencies. To do that, a type of statistical multivariate analysis—probit analysis—is necessary.[10] In a probit model, one tests how an explanatory factor affects the probability that the tenderer will win the contract and at the same time controls for other factors that are likely to influence the outcome.[11] For example, let us say that A is hypothesized to affect C, but C is also expected to be influenced by B. By using a multivariate analysis and including control variables, one tries to separate both of these effects.

The results of the multivariate analysis are shown in Table 6.9. For a more detailed technical description of the multivariate analysis, see Svensson (1998).[12] There are two main ways to measure the strength of the relationship between an explanatory factor and the outcome. First, the relationship can be tested for statistical significance. Here, one normally claims that the relationship should be statistically significant with 95% confidence, or at least 90%. Second, quantitative effects can be measured. More precisely one can ask, How is the probability to win the tender affected by a small change in an explanatory variable? I will only calculate quantitative effects for explanatory variables that have a significant impact on the outcome.

The first group of explanatory factors, general experiences of the tenderer, does not seem to have any influence at all on the outcome. As was suggested above, the experience with the host country and with similar assignments abroad are more important for the prequalification and invitation. The result that the general experience of the tenderer has no impact on the outcome is not surprising, because the tenderer has in the second competitive step submitted a proposal with more detailed information about the employees' experience and the composition of the team, and so forth. Turning to the second group of explanatory factors, both the education level and international experience of the team leader have, on the other hand, a significant influence, as expected, with at least 90% confidence in the outcome. In quantitative terms, the probability of being awarded the assignment increases by approximately 5 to 8 percentile units when the team leader's education or international experience increases by three years.

The third group of factors, long-term relationship factors, has the strongest

---

[10] Since the dependent variable is qualitative in nature and equals 1 if the tenderer wins the tender and 0 if he or she loses it, a probit model is an appropriate statistical model to use.

[11] Such control factors are not only those factors described in Table 6.2 above, but also "dummy" variables representing unobservable factors that we cannot measure.

[12] As a goodness-of-fit test for the whole model's ability to predict the outcome of tender evaluation, I calculate the percentages of correctly predicted observations for the whole sample and for the small group of observations for outcome, that is, for awarded tenders. For the whole sample, 70% to 75% of the observations are correctly predicted which is clearly acceptable. For the group of awarded tenders, 50% to 55% are correctly predicted. The latter figure should not be compared to a "random" share of 50%, but to the actual share of awarded tenders of 37%. Thus, the model also predicts the outcome of the tender evaluation very well also according to the latter goodness-of-fit test.

Table 6.9. The influence of different factors on the outcome of the tender evaluation by probit analysis.

Dependent variable: the outcome of a tender document (Awarded=1; Lost=0).
Statistical model: probit model.

Explanatory factors	Statistical significance of the relationship	Quantitative effect on the outcome in percentile units
Experience with similar assignments abroad (number)	0	--
Experience with the host country (yes/no)	0	--
Team leader's degree of education (3 years)	* / **	6-8
Team leader's international experience (3-4 years)	* / **	5-7
Previous experience with the client (yes/no)	***	20-25
Visits to the client (yes/no)	**	12-15
Local office in the host country (yes/no)	**	15-20
Permanent office (yes/no)	** / ***	18-22
Representative office (yes/no)	* / **	12-15
Cooperation with international CFs (yes/no)	0	--
Cooperation with local CFs (percent)	0	--

Note: Number of observations equals 316. The relationships are positive if nothing else is stated. ***, ** and * mean that the relationship is statistically significant with 99%, 95% and 90% confidence, respectively. A "0" indicates that the relationship is not statistically significant. If two alternative significance levels are shown for a specific explanatory variable, then the significance level varies across the specification of the model. Quantitative effects are only calculated for explanatory variables that have a statistically significant impact on the outcome. The information in the parentheses shows how the quantitative effects on the probability should be related to changes in the explanatory variables. For example, if the team leader's education level increases by three years, the probability of obtaining the assignment increases by approximately 6 to 8 percentile units, or if the CF has had previous contracts for a client compared to if it has not, then the probability increases by 20 to 25 percentile units.

influence on the outcome for significance level. Previous contracts for the client have an impact on the outcome with at least 99% confidence, and they increase the probability of winning the contract with 20 to 25 percentile units on average. This proves that repeat purchases are common in the consulting sectors, although several CFs are allowed to compete. A visit to the client in connection to the tender also has a significant impact on the outcome and it increases the probability of winning the contract by 12 to 15 percentile units.

One can make several observations about the visit's impact on the outcome.

First, the statistical estimations show that a visit has a positive impact on the probability of winning the contract irrespective of whether the tenderer had previous contracts for the client or not. Second, one can test why the tenderer visits the client. The tenderer can visit the client: 1) to affect the client in some way in his or her decision making, for example, to market the firm's ability or to develop long-term relationships with the client; or 2) to find a source information about the project, client or host country, so that a better proposal can be submitted. If the first hypothesis is true, then the visit would only have an impact on the outcome when the client may influence the evaluation. If the second hypothesis is true, however, then the visits would have an influence on the probability of winning the contract irrespective of whether the client is allowed to influence the evaluation or not. The estimations in Svensson (1999) indicate that the visits are most important when the client is allowed to influence the evaluation. Thus, the first hypothesis seems to be true, and the second seems to be false. When multilateral development agencies assist with the financing of the project, the client is sometimes not allowed to influence the tender evaluation. This is the case when EU-TACIS and EU-ALA are involved and when AsDB gives technical assistance to the client and makes preproject purchases.

Also local presence in the form of an office seems to have a positive impact on the outcome. The relationship is stronger for permanent offices compared to representative offices, both for statistical significance and for quantitative effects. Thus, a permanent office is associated with a higher expected payoff, but, as was discussed in Chapter 3, is also associated with a higher risk than a representative office—especially in emerging markets where demand is unstable and unpredictable. Cooperation with other international and local CFs fails, however, to show any significant relationship with the outcome. This may depend on that the client or financier forces all tenderers in a project to suggest cooperation with local CFs and, in the case of international CFs, whether the tenderer must cooperate because of being very specialized, or because competition is hard.

The statistical estimations show that large projects are more difficult to win than small projects, because then more firms compete, or are allowed to compete. The competitors will undertake more strategies and use more competitive factors when the tender value is high to get scope economies. Each strategic factor will then be worth less for the larger project. Combined strategies and competitive factors will therefore be necessary in order to win large contracts.

One must also analyze whether the determinants of the outcome vary across financing groups, because these groups have different rules for procurement of consulting services. The same four financing groups are used as in the analysis of the first competitive step in Section 6.2. The groups include projects financed by Sida, EU funds and other multilateral development agencies (World Bank, regional development banks, etc.) as well as commercial projects. These groups have 106, 45, 87 and 78 observations, respectively. The estimations for individual financing groups are shown in Table 6.10. Since there are less observations in each group, the uncertainty in the estimations will be higher, implying that the significance levels will be lower than for the basic estimates in Table 6.9. Not surprisingly, the Sida group, which has more than 100 observations, is also the group whose estimates have the highest significance levels.

There are *significant* differences across financiers for four explanatory variables. The experience of the team leader has clearly a stronger relationship with the outcome for Sida-financed projects than for the other groups, whereas the opposite is true for the team leader's education level. The long-term relationship factors have a more positive influence on the probability for Sida, EU and commercial projects compared to projects financed by other multilateral development agencies. Generally, commercial projects do not differ significantly from the Sida and EU groups apart from the characteristics of the team leader. The differences are, in fact, at least as large between Sida and the other development agency groups as between commercial projects and any of the three development agency groups.

Both long-term relationship factors have a positive influence on the outcome for Sida and in the most cases also for EU and commercial projects. The local office exerts a positive impact only on the probability of winning the contract for Sida projects and partly for the commercial group. For the multilateral group, only the education level of the team leader seems to be a relevant factor for the outcome. Many key persons employed by the CFs who I spoke with when collecting the database claim that Sida primarily gives priority to the experience of the employees, whereas multilateral development agencies favor the education level of the employees. This is supported in the statistical estimations. The reason may be that Sida has more experience and knowledge about Swedish firms and their employees, and can therefore better evaluate the experience of these employees, but multilateral development agencies must compare the education levels across tender documents. The weak explanatory power for the group of other multilateral development agencies (only one variable is statistically significant) may depend on the fact that these agencies have stricter rules for procurement and that these rules are followed more consistently in the evaluations. It may also depend on this group being the most heterogenous one of the four groups. The Sida, EU and commercial groups are relatively homogenous for tender procedures. A further division of the group of other multilateral development agencies into subgroups like the World Bank, AsDB, EBRD, and so on, is inhibited by the fact that these subgroups would have too few observations.

Table 6.10. The influence of different factors on the outcome of the tender evaluation across financing groups.

Dependent variable: the outcome of a tender document (Awarded=1; Lost=0).
Statistical model: probit model.

Explanatory factors	Financing groups				Statistical significant differences between groups?
	Sida	EU funds	Multilateral	Commercial	
Experience with similar assignments abroad	0	0	0	* (neg.)	No
Experience with the host country	0	0	0	0	No
Team leader's degree of education	0	*	**	*	Sida vs multilateral
Team leader's international experience	***	0	0	0	Sida vs other three groups
Previous experience with the client	**	***	0	*	Multilateral vs other three groups
Visits to the client	***	*	0	*	Multilateral vs other three groups
Local office in the host country	***	0	0	*	No
Cooperation with international CFs	0	0	0	0	No
Cooperation with local CFs	0	0	0	0	No
Number of observations	106	45	87	78	xxx

Note: The relationships are positive if nothing else is stated. ***, ** and * mean that the relationship is statistically significant with 99, 95 and 90% confidence, respectively. A "0" indicates that the relationship is not statistically significant.

6.3.4 Interpretations, Consequences and Policy Implications

When interpreting the results of the statistical estimations in the second competitive step, for example, that factor X has a significant impact on the selection of supplier, one must remember that factor X is important for the final selection *given that the CF has the minimum experience or competence needed to be invited or short-listed.* As was seen in the multivariate estimations, the long-term relationship factors have at least as strong explanatory power on the outcome of the tender evaluations as traditional experience and skill factors of the firms and their staff. This was the case for commercial projects as well as for projects financed by Sida and EU. Remarkably, the long-term relationship factors are given zero points in the tender evaluations of Sida and EU funds.[13] For these three financing groups, it is therefore possible that the client in some (but far from all) of the tenders has already decided from the beginning which supplier to select. This phenomenon is also called "procurement with a hidden agenda". There are two reasons for the client to invite several CFs to compete for the tender, even though the selection is pre-decided. First, the client may be forced to use competitive procurement by the financier (for projects financed by development agencies) or by the law (for commercial projects). Second, a CF may have developed strong long-term relationships with the client in previously implemented projects and the CF knows that the client trusts him or her. The client is, however, afraid that this CF will try to use its position and thereby charge a higher fee. By inviting several CFs to tender, the client can expose the old CF to competitive pressure (for commercial projects). If the preselected CF does not submit an apparently bad proposal, then this firm will definitely be selected. Pre-decided selections can, however, only explain some of the strong explanatory power of the long-term relationship factors.

A complementary explanation is that if several proposals are similar in quality, it is understandable that the client chooses a CF with which he or she has experience, because the quality of the services and the cooperation between the CF and the client can seldom be evaluated a priori. Furthermore, because the development agencies during recent years have allowed the client to participate in the selection of a supplier, it is not surprising that the evaluations have become similar to those in the commercial market. It may even be in the interest of the financier that the relationship between the client and the CF runs smoothly and that all parties are satisfied. Previous relationships between the CF and the client may then unofficially be allowed to determine the selection of

---

[13] As was concluded in Chapter 4, Sida neither seems to follow the procurement rules for negotiated contracts, where most of the negotiated contracts had a contract value above the upper limit of 0.2 MSEK.

supplier.

Since the results indicate that the development agencies, especially Sida and the EU funds, do not follow their strict tender rules, a policy implication is that these agencies can either skip, or at least relax, their rules, or strengthen the sanctions associated with violations of the rules. If the rules are relaxed, the development agency should, however, still assist the client with preproject identification, negotiations and postproject evaluation, because the knowledge gap and thereby the difference in bargaining power is large between CFs from developed countries and clients in emerging markets. Otherwise, it is likely that the CFs will suggest projects that are profitable for themselves rather than for the client, or try to cheat the client in some other way.

Another conclusion in the multivariate analysis is that Sida gives priority to the international experience of the professionals employed by the CFs and does not take the education level of the professionals into account, whereas EU funds and other multilateral development agencies, in contrast, give priority to the education level of the staff. The advantage of giving priority to the education level is that highly educated professionals in general are capable of learning faster and to a higher level than less educated professionals. Sida's policy, which focuses solely on experience, has three main implications for the (Swedish) consulting sector. First, it will be less profitable to invest heavily in education in Sweden. In fact, Swedish CFs seem to have difficulties in recruiting doctors or other highly educated professionals. If the pattern to give no weight to the education level also is true when other Swedish government authorities procure services (which is not unlikely), then it may partly explain why Sweden lags behind other developed countries for education level attained, including the number of PhD graduates.

Second, a monotonous focus on the experience of the staff will also inhibit the regrowth in the capacity of professionals in the home country. In tender evaluations, a 50-year-old professional will win out over a 40-year-old professional, who in turn will come ahead of a 30-year-old professional. This means that the coming generation of professionals employed in CFs will be restrained from entering the international market. Not surprisingly, a disproportionally large number of Swedish professionals (especially team leaders) who participate in international projects are age 50 years and up. Third, the employees in Swedish CFs, who certainly are well experienced, will not have the required characteristics when multilateral development agencies procure consulting services. This means that Sida's role as a spearhead for Swedish CFs into the market financed by multilateral development agencies will be limited.

6.4 Negotiated Contracts

As in the case of the first competitive step, one would preferably have information on projects where the firm is invited as well as on those where it is not invited when analyzing negotiated contracts. An alternative analysis can be undertaken by comparing the characteristics and underlying factors of negotiated contracts with those characteristics of proposals submitted in competition. In Table 6.11, averages for plausible factors are described for negotiated contracts as well as tenders in competition. In fact, there is only one major difference between the two groups of tenders. It seems that long-term relationship factors and repeat purchases are even more important for negotiated contracts than for tenders in competition. In negotiations, the CF had experience with the client in 69% of the cases (which of course is 100% for continued negotiated contracts), but this share was only 35% for tenders in competition.

There are, however, alternative hypotheses. One can expect firms that are

Figure 6.2. The relationship between success ratio for tenders in competition and negotiated contracts as a proportion of all awarded contracts for Swedish CFs in percent of contract values.

Negotiated contracts divided by all awarded contracts (%)

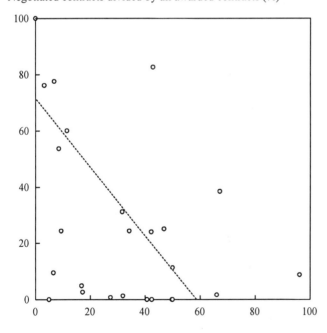

Note: Number of observations equals 26. The dashed line is a statistical estimate (regression estimate) of the linear relationship between the variables on the vertical and horizontal axis.

Table 6.11. Explanatory factors for negotiated contracts and comparisons with tenders in competition in averages of number, years and percent.

Explanatory factors	Negotiated contracts			Tenders in competition		
	New	Continued	All	Won	Lost	All
The firm's experience with similar projects abroad (number)	12.1	12.1	12.1	11.9	10.4	10.9
The firm's experience with the host country (percent)	69	100	77	77	71	73
Team-leader's education (years)	5.3	5.9	5.5	6.5	6.1	6.2
Team-leader's foreign experience (years)	8.0	10.1	8.6	10.1	8.9	9.3
Previous experience with the client (percent)	60	100	69	44	30	35
Visits to the client (percent)	71	80	74	75	66	69
Local offices in the host country (percent)	21	16	20	24	14	18

weak and have a low performance when tendering in competition to be forced to use other channels to obtain contracts. On the other hand, firms that use nego-tiated contracts mostly will be less skilled in designing and specifying proposals in competition and in learning tender rules specifically for each development agency. This implies that the causality between these factors is unsettled. Figure 6.2 shows a plot between negotiated contracts as a percentage of all awarded contracts, and awarded tenders in competition as a percentage of all tenders in competition at the firm level—with both percentages measured for tender values. The relationship is clearly negative. To measure the linear relationship between the two variables, a Pearson correlation coefficient is estimated. This test gives a coefficient of -0.46 which is statistically significant with 95% confidence.[14]

6.5 Summary

In this chapter, competitive factors and strategies influencing the outcome of international tender evaluations have been analyzed. When consulting services are procured in competition there are two competitive steps. First, some CFs are invited to participate in the tender, either with or without application. In the second step, the invited CFs may submit a tender document if they wish. There-after, the client will, together with the financier, evaluate the proposals and choose one of the tenderers. General experiences of the whole firm, experience with the host country and the client, and experiences with similar assignments abroad seem to determine which CFs are invited to tender. Although these factors are significant across all financing alternatives, the more the client is allowed to influence the short-listing or invitation, the more important these factors become.

When detailed proposals are submitted in the second step, other factors determine the outcome of the tender evaluation. Here, long-term relationships between the supplier and the client seem to be the most important determinants, for example, previous contracts for the client (repeat purchases) or whether the CF visited the client or not. Previous contracts for the client may increase the probability of winning the contract by as much as 20 to 25 percentile units. It can also be concluded that the CF visits the client to affect the decision making rather than as a source of information about the project so that a better proposal

---

[14] -1 means a maximal negative relationship and 0 means no relationship at all. The plot and correlation will be similar if we compare the *number* of negotiated contracts as a share of all awarded contracts with the *number* of awarded tenders in competition as a share of all tenders in competition *instead of tender and contract values*. The estimated correlation coefficient is then -0.41, statistically significant with 95% confidence.

can be submitted. The experience and education level of the team leader also have significant impacts on the firm's probability of winning the contract. Local presence in the form of a local office, especially a permanent one, has a strong positive influence on the outcome. However, general experience factors of the whole firm, such as the experience with the host country or with similar projects abroad, do not have any significant impact on the outcome in the second step.

There are some differences across financing alternatives. Sida gives priority to the experience of the proposed staff, whereas the other development agencies and the client seem to favor the education level. A consequence is that the re-growth of professionals in Sweden will be inhibited and Sida's role in spear-heading the Swedish CFs in new markets will be limited because multilateral development agencies require other skills of the staff than what Sida requires. Long-term relationships are important for commercial, Sida and EU projects but not for projects financed by other multilateral development agencies. The latter agencies seem to have stricter rules for procurement of consulting services. Notably, the long-term relationship factors are given zero points in the tender evaluations of the development agencies. All in all, the differences between the three development agency groups are at least as large as those between commercial projects and any of these agency groups.

The fact that the long-term relationship factors have at least as large an influence on the outcome as the experience and competence of the firm and its staff is an indication that in some (but far from all) of the projects the client has pre-decided which supplier to choose. The client invites several CFs to tender anyway for two reasons. First, the client may be forced to do so by the financier. Second, the client wants to subject an old CF to competitive pressure. Since many of the development agencies do not seem to follow their strict tender rules, a policy implication is that these agencies can either skip, or at least relax, their strict rules, or increase the sanctions associated with violations of the rules.

Regarding negotiated contracts, previous experience of the client and thereby repeat purchases are even more prominent than for projects procured in competition. Firms that have a low success ratio for tenders in competition have many negotiated contracts as a share of all awarded contracts. However, it has not been settled whether this depends on firms that are too weak to tender for projects in competition are forced to use negotiations in order to win contracts, or because firms that give priority to negotiations become less skilled to design and specify proposals in competition. Finally, I expect that the analysis and conclusions in this chapter are valid not only for CFs operating in the infrastructure sectors, but also for CFs operating in other sectors such as the health, educational, juridical and computer sectors. The reason is that the latter CFs and their services have in principle the same characteristics as the former CFs and their services.

Chapter 7

MANAGEMENT SERVICES AND STATE-OWNED CONSULTING FIRMS

One of the purposes of this chapter is to analyze the trend from engineering services toward management services in the international market. I examine the sectors and financing alternatives in which this trend is most pronounced and discuss the consequences for the consulting firms (CFs). The adaptation to this trend for private CFs can be inhibited by the presence of state-owned CFs, which are affiliates of government authorities or infrastructure operators. Whether or not these state-owned CFs have an unfair competitive advantage compared with privately owned CFs is also examined.

7.1 Engineering versus Management Services

In recent years, multidisciplinary projects have become more frequent abroad. In these projects, the CFs are required not only to supply traditional engineering services such as, for example, master plans, feasibility studies, and design, procurement and supervision services, but also management services in the form of training, institutional building, and operation services as well as reorganization and tariff studies. In this context, management services means services that are specific for the infrastructure sectors, and not services that can be supplied by McKinsey, BCG or similar CFs. The main reason for the trend toward management services in the international market is, of course, that inexpensive local technical consulting firms (TCFs) and engineers today have learned more about how to implement the technical calculations and the design themselves, but they still lack the competence to organize, supervise and plan the projects and to supply procurement services. As concluded in Chapter 5, the increased training of local CFs and alliances between international and local CFs during the last decade have facilitated knowledge transfer to emerging markets. The services easiest to learn for the local CFs have been technical design and calculation services. As a consequence, the price competition for technical design services has become tougher for international TCFs. Furthermore, there have been worldwide trends toward privatization of state-owned entities and deregulation of markets in the infrastructure sectors. In emerging markets, the (former) state-owned operators are often ineffective, corrupt and seldom ready to supply utilities (e.g., electricity, phone rentals, railway travels) in a competitive market. They need, in other words, a great deal of reorganization to become more effective when operating the plants or systems.

As a result of these facts and trends, the development agencies have, during the last decade, changed the composition of consulting services that they procure from firms in developed countries. First, in the case of investments, technical calculations and design are to a higher degree purchased from local TCFs and engineers, whereas services purchased from international CFs aim more to facilitate knowledge transfer to the host country and to coordinate, support and train local TCFs and engineers. Second, management services are now procured more frequently from international CFs to make the operation of the systems or plants more effective. These management services can take several directions. For example, engineers or economists from developed countries are placed in ministries in the host countries to supply institutional building and support services to the clients, infrastructure operators in the host country are reorganized, government entities are oriented to the market, and tariff studies are initiated. Whether the improved technical skills of the local TCFs are good enough so that they can do the technical calculations and the design themselves is not clear and has not been evaluated by the development agencies or anybody else, but these agencies seem to believe that the local TCFs are qualified.

In Table 7.1, the services supplied by CFs and included in my questionnaire (see Appendix B) are divided into three groups: 1) technical design services, 2) technical support services, and 3) management services. The motivation for the division of engineering services is that the design services include drawings and technical calculations, whereas the support services are related to organizational skills, supervision and logistics.[1] Competition from local TCFs has become stronger in the technical design services group. An important observation is that technical design services are mostly supplied as documents (feasibility studies, preliminary and detailed design), whereas technical support and management services are mainly supplied as labor services (supervision, commissioning, project management, training, institutional building, operation services). Services supplied as documents can to a higher degree be produced in the home country of the CF.

To simplify our understanding of the services provided by CFs, we can think about two theoretical CFs—a traditional and a modern CF—that do not need to exist in their pure forms in the real world. A traditional CF supplies all kinds of

---

[1] Feasibility studies include both technical and economic calculations and could, therefore, be placed in either the design or the support group. Technical calculations account for the largest part and feasibility studies are therefore placed in the former group. Classification as the support group would not, however, have changed the results of the empirical analysis in this chapter significantly.

Table 7.1. Classification of services supplied by CFs.

| Group | Engineering services | | Management services |
	Technical design services	Technical support services	
Services	Feasibility study	Master or development plan	Institutional building
	Preliminary design	Procurement	Training or education
	Detailed design	Supervision of construction	Reorganization study
		Project management	Tariff study
		Commissioning	Operation services

Note: A feasibility study includes mostly both technical and economical calculations and could either be placed in the design or support group. Technical calculations account, in general, for the largest part and feasibility study is therefore placed in the design group.

engineering services but no management services. In contrast, a modern CF supplies technical support and management services, but design and technical calculations have been dropped. These two kinds of CFs thus compete with each other in technical support services. The modern CF can, in fact, be seen as a combined technical and management CF. In reality, however, most CFs operating in the infrastructure sectors supply all three types of services.

Table 7.2 shows how frequent the three groups of services are in the projects that Swedish CFs tendered for between 1995 and 1997—both for number of tenders and for tender values. In this instance, I am most interested in tender values (the second column), where the tenders are weighted with the contract value in MSEK. Only one group of services is included in 50% of the tenders, but 50% of the tenders have a combination of two or three of the groups. More than 40% of the tenders have only design or management services. The support services group is the least common group on its own, but it is more common in combination with the other two groups. Not surprisingly, the combination of design and management services is rare. All in all, the tenders in the sample include some kind of technical design, support or management services in 54%, 58% and 46%, respectively, of all cases when weighted with tender values.[2] When considering the number of tenders (first column), the pattern is similar, but tenders that comprise one group of services have a higher percentage of the total (64% instead of 50%). This implies that tenders with combined services, on average, have larger contract values than tenders that include only one group of services.

The period of measurement, 1995 to 1997, is too short to permit analysis of the composition of services over time. General opinion is, however, that 10 or

---

[2] For example, the figure of 54% for design services is calculated as 19% + 26% + 1% + 8%.

Table 7.2. Combination of services included in contracts that Swedish CFs tendered for between 1995 and 1997 in percent.

Services included in the contract	All tenders (n=358)	
	% of number of tenders	% of tender values
Only technical design services	24	19
Only technical support services	11	9
Only management services	29	22
Technical design and support services	14	26
Technical design and management services	4	1
Technical support and management services	12	15
All three groups of services	6	8
Total	100	100

15 years ago technical design and support services were included almost exclusively in international projects. This was especially the case for Swedish TCFs with assignments in the Middle East in the 1980s. As much as 85% to 95% and 70% to 80% of all projects could then include some kind of design services and support services, respectively, whereas the corresponding figure for management services could be 5% to 10%. An interesting analysis can, however, be done across financing groups, as shown in Figure 7.1. I estimated the share of the three groups of services in each tender.[3] Thereafter, I calculated a weighted average of tender values for each financing group (as in Table 7.2).[4]

On average, design, support and management services have 36%, 32% and 32%, respectively, of the total tender values. It is obvious that the composition of services in the projects differs across financing groups. As expected, develop-

---

[3] In the database, we know which type of services are included in each tender, but not how the tender value is distributed among these services. Therefore, we have used the following method to estimate the percentages of design, support and management services in a specific tender. Each type of service is given a weight corresponding to its share of the total number of services in the tender. For example, in a project that includes feasibility study, supervision, procurement and training, a 25% weight has been given to design services, 50% to support services and 25% to management services. When only one group of services is represented in a project, 100% of those services have of course been given to that group. This method may imply that some types of services that, in general, have a high turnover (e.g., detailed design) are underestimated in the statistics; that is, the percentages for our three groups may be biased. The relationship across financing groups is, however, not expected to be biased in a systematic and serious way.

[4] It should be noted that the percentages in Figure 7.1 correspond to the projects that Swedish CFs have tendered for and not all projects for which a specific group of development agencies assists with financing.

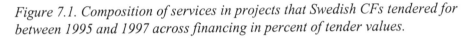

Figure 7.1. Composition of services in projects that Swedish CFs tendered for between 1995 and 1997 across financing in percent of tender values.

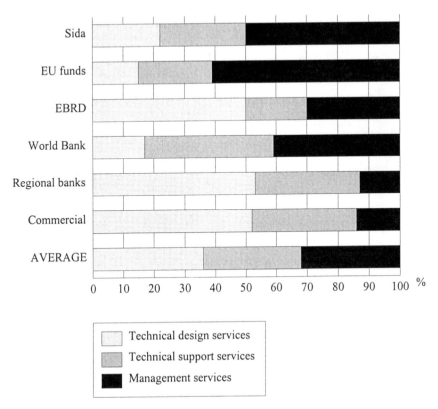

ment agencies especially have a high share of management services and a low share of design services. The EU funds are the most extreme where management services account for about 60% of the total, but also Sida and the World Bank have around 50% and 40%, respectively, of management services. The difference between the World Bank and the regional development banks is here somewhat unexpected. It could be explained by that regional development banks to a higher degree assist with technical assistance in the precontract phase, which includes more design services. The World Bank, on the other hand, assists to a larger extent with subsidized loans in the implementation phase of investment projects, and loans to restructuring projects, which are more connected with support and management services. Furthermore, commercial projects have by tradition been more focused on large investment projects with design services.

In Figure 7.2, a similar distribution for the three groups of services is descri-

Figure 7.2. Composition of services in projects that Swedish CFs tendered for between 1995 and 1997 by sector in percent of tender values.

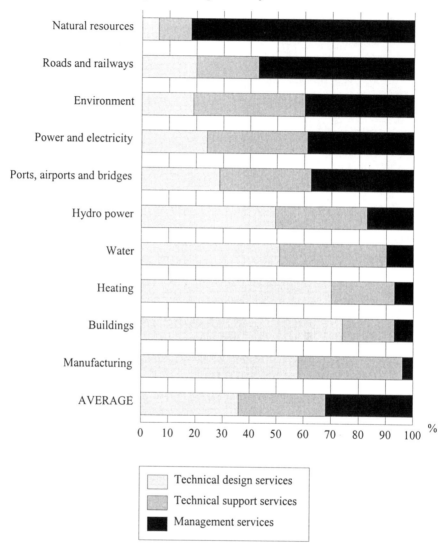

bed across sectors.[5] Natural resources and roads and railways are the sectors where the trend toward management services has gone the furthest. None of these sectors has more than 20% of the total as design services. Environment, power and electricity, and ports, airports and bridges are in the middle of the

---

[5] The telecom sector is not shown, because I wish to keep the composition of services in Swedtel's projects a secret.

Table 7.3. Combination of services included in awarded and lost tenders that Swedish CFs competed for between 1995 and 1997 in percent.

Services included in the project	Awarded tenders (n=135)		Lost tenders (n=223)	
	% of number of tenders	% of tender values	% of number of tenders	% of tender values
Only design services	25	18	24	19
Only support services	12	10	11	8
Only management services	29	29	29	20
Design and support services	12	17	15	29
Design and management services	4	1	3	1
Support and management services	12	15	13	15
All three groups of services	6	10	5	8
Total	100	100	100	100

distribution. In the hydro power, manufacturing, building, heating and water sectors, management services account mostly for less than 10% of the total and design services for around 50% to 70%. Thus, in these sectors it is still possible for the Swedish TCFs to export their traditional engineering services. One can also, however, expect a shift toward management services in these sectors, especially in the heating and water sectors, where there is a need for tariff and reorganization studies as well as market orienting of state-owned operators in emerging markets. It is in the latter two sectors where local TCFs and engineers seem to lag behind in design services.

In Table 7.3, I expand the figures from Table 7.2 and analyze whether or not there are any differences between awarded and lost tenders. For number of tenders (columns 1 and 3), the awarded and lost tenders include approximately the same percentages of the three service groups. When considering tender values (columns 2 and 4), however, tenders with only management services account for 29% of the awarded tenders, but only 20% of the lost tenders. Another significant difference is the combination of design and support services that are included in 17% of the awarded and 29% of the lost tenders. Of the awarded tenders, 46%, 52% and 55% include some kind of design, support and management services, respectively. The corresponding figures for lost tenders are 57%, 60% and 44%. A conclusion would be that the competition for projects in the international market that include design and support services is more fierce than it is for projects that include management services.

In Figure 7.3, I compare awarded and lost tenders for different financing alternatives. On average, awarded tenders include 30%, 32% and 38% of design,

Figure 7.3. Composition of services in awarded and lost tenders that Swedish CFs competed for between 1995 and 1997 across financing in percent of tender values.

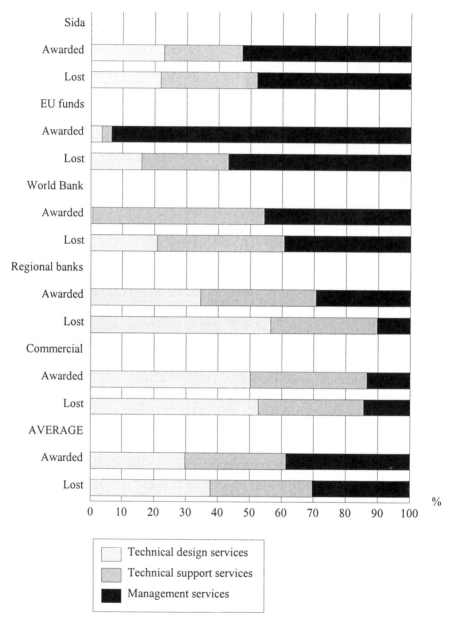

support and management services, and the corresponding figures for lost tenders are 37%, 33% and 30%, respectively. Not surprisingly, the differences for Sida-financed projects are insignificant. For all three groups of multilateral develop-

Figure 7.4. Composition of services in awarded and lost tenders that Swedish CFs competed for between 1995 and 1997 by sector in percent of tender values.

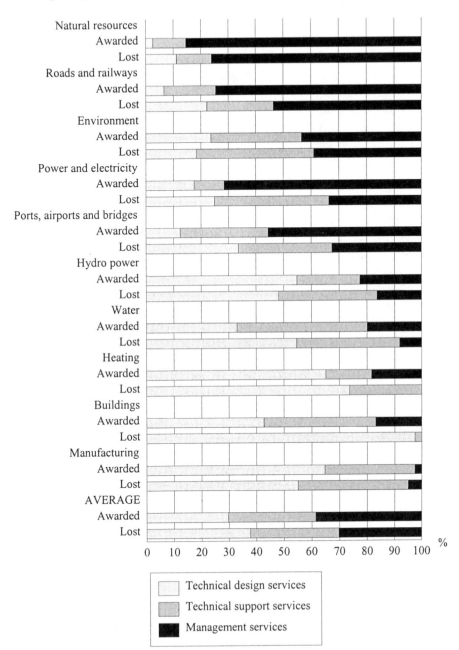

ment agencies, awarded tenders clearly include fewer design services and more management services than do lost tenders. This indicates that competition from other international and local CFs for design services is very stiff when multi-lateral development agencies are involved.

Similar distributions for awarded and lost tenders across sectors are shown in Figure 7.4. The differences in preference for management services in awarded compared with lost tenders are the largest in the roads and railways, power and electricity, ports, airports and bridges, water, heating and building sectors. There are also some differences in the natural resource and hydro power sectors, whereas the other sectors show a more equal or even an opposite pattern.

7.2 Consequences of the Trend toward Management Services

The trend from design toward management services has several consequences for the international CFs—especially the TCFs. The new kinds of services will, of course, require other skills and experiences of the TCFs' employees. Either the TCFs have to further educate their employees or recruit a new type of pro-fessional who is able to supply management services. In this area, the Swedish privately owned TCFs seem to lag behind their competitors in other countries. One problem is that most of the private TCFs have permanent employees and are heavily focused on design services. Together with strict labor market regula-tions in Sweden, this problem makes it difficult to address necessary reorganiza-tions of the personnel structure. Of the private CFs included in the sample, it is only the management consultants Hifab, ISO, NCG and SPM that are fully adapted for the new trend toward management services. Swedish TCFs that lack the ability to acquire management skills will soon be driven out of business abroad. Some of the Swedish private TCFs, whose operations are heavily based on design services, have already slowed down their foreign activities. As I will show in the next section, the backwardness of the Swedish privately owned TCFs depends partly on the existence of state-owned CFs in Sweden.

Compared with design services, exports of support and management services require that the CFs' employees spend a larger part of their time with the client in the host country. As noted earlier, management services are to a higher degree supplied as labor services compared with design services, which mostly are supplied in document form. As technical support and management services become more important at the expense of design services, the CFs' costs for offices at home will be lower; at the same time, reimbursements in the form of travels, subsistence allowances and temporary offices in the host country will increase. Direct contact and cooperation with clients will also be more frequent, which emphasizes the need for social competence and good communication between the CFs' employees and the client. The trend toward management services, often jointly produced, will give another important implication. The knowledge transfer to the host countries can be expected to be intensified because the direct contact between the transferors and transferees becomes more frequent.

The technical design services may still be controlled by the international CF when investments are planned, but a larger part of these services will be subcontracted to inexpensive local TCFs. Subcontracting means that the international CF to a larger extent depends on cooperation with local partners. This can either be achieved by cooperating temporarily but recurrently with local TCFs on a project basis, or by establishing or acquiring local permanent offices. In the latter case, one has to remember the high risk of owning permanent offices in markets with volatile and unpredictable demand. If any permanent office is established or acquired at all, then a minority-owned office should be chosen (see Chapter 3). The international CF must then assure itself that it can quickly exit the ownership, or suspend the office, if the host country demand falls unexpectedly. Temporary cooperation may therefore be the best alternative.

The subcontracting will, however, make it more difficult to achieve scope economies. Since a larger share of the services are supplied by local engineers, fixed costs associated with a specific client or project, for example, travel and contract costs, will be spread across a smaller sales volume for the international CF. To achieve some scope economies, information costs must therefore be minimized. This means that a closer integration and cooperation with the local engineers will be necessary, where information flows between the local and international CFs must be frictionless. In this situation, it will probably be advantageous to cooperate with the same local TCF over time.

There has, historically, been a strong interdependence between TCFs and contractors originating from the same country (Svensson, 1997). The fact that TCFs from developed countries supply fewer engineering services, especially design and procurement services, in connection with investment projects abroad means that this interdependence has become weaker during the last decade. Fifteen years ago in the Middle East, Swedish TCFs cooperated with Swedish contractors on a regular basis. Today, this interaction occurs less often. For example, only 10 of 458 proposals in the database were submitted to a client in a consortium with a contractor, and not more than 18 of 458 proposals were submitted directly to a contractor that already had a contract for a client.

There are several ways for the CFs to respond to the trend toward management services, and local CFs have learned to implement many of the technical components of the projects themselves. In principle, three different strategies have developed in the international consulting market: 1) Specialization in the most advanced engineering services with a small inclusion of management services and subcontracting the bulk of design services to local TCFs. Knowledge upgrading of engineering skills and supply of IT services will be very important when applying this strategy (examples in the Swedish sample: SWECO and ÅF); 2) A multidisciplinary strategy where the firm supplies technical support and management services. Technical design services have in this instance completely been dropped (examples in the sample: Hifab International, SweRoad); and 3) A pure management strategy. No engineering services are then supplied (examples in the sample: SwedeRail, Swedavia, NCG, SPM).

As a result of the new trend in the international consulting market, management and accounting consultants who have not operated in the infrastructure sectors earlier (e.g., Andersen Consulting, Cooper & Lybrands and Ernst & Young), have the opportunity to penetrate the market financed by development agencies. The services supplied by these firms have mainly been operation and reorganization services and market orienting of government entities (i.e., they have applied strategy 3, described earlier). In the first place, these firms compete for projects financed by EBRD and EU and not Sida-financed projects. The reason is that they charge a fee per hour that is higher than Sida's maximum fee.

As local CFs continue to learn how to replicate services implemented by international CFs, it is expected that local CFs also will be able to supply management services in the future and that the trend toward new and more complex services demanded in the international market has only begun. Thus, in 10 years, there may be other even more sophisticated services, which are the crucial services that the international CFs must be able to supply to be competitive in the international market.

7.3 Privately Owned versus State-Owned CFs

The Swedish infrastructure consulting sector is characterized by state-owned CFs, here called "Swed-firms," that operate in the international market. In 1996, the Swed-firms accounted for as much as 47% of the total exports of the CFs in the sample (see Table A.3 in Appendix A). This is a unique Swedish phenomenon. Certainly, state-owned CFs exist also in other European countries, for example, Denmark and France, but the foreign state-owned CFs have only a few percent of the total consulting exports in their countries. Historically, the Swed-firms have supplied management services to a much higher degree than have the private CFs and the two groups of CFs have thus competed in different segments of the infrastructure market. This is logical because the Swed-firms are owned by large Swedish state-owned operators in the infrastructure sectors that have huge human capital resources and thereby know how to operate and reorganize a system or a plant.

As a result of the trend toward management services, the private CFs have

Figure 7.5. Composition of services in projects that Swedish CFs tendered for between 1995 and 1997 by firm group in percent of tender values.

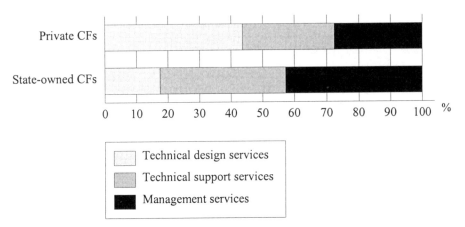

been forced to enter the market in which the Swed-firms operate. When considering the composition of services in the projects that the CFs tendered for in Figure 7.5, there is still a substantial difference between the two groups. Projects that private CFs tendered for include 44% of design services, whereas support and management services account for around 28% each. The corresponding figures for the Swed-firms are 17%, 40% and 43%.[6] This pattern is not surprising, because the skills required for many of those management services demanded by the development agencies can be found among professionals employed by state-owned operators and government authorities in Sweden, for example, in the sectors for aviation, road security, statistics, land surveying and government administration services.

The Swedish private CFs have had problems adapting themselves to the management trend irrespective of which (if any) of the three suggested strategies in the previous section they have tried to apply. Interesting issues to examine are whether the existence of Swed-firms has prevented this adaptation and whether the Swed-firms enjoy a privileged position in the market compared with the private CFs. To analyze these issues, one has to find out under which different conditions private and state-owned CFs operate. In this analysis, I have two starting points, or essential characteristics, of CFs: 1) Since CFs sell services on a project basis and offer the clients flexibility, one of the largest problems for the CFs to solve is matching resources (professionals) available with the demand for services; and 2) Since the only factor of production is the professionals who implement the services, and since it is likely that the long-term relationships

---

[6] The Swed-firms included in the sample are Swedavia, SwedeRail, SwedPower, Swedtel and SweRoad.

Table 7.4. Terms of employment and exclusive right to professionals in private and state-owned CFs.

	Exclusive right to professionals	No exclusive right to professionals
Hired professionals and variable wage costs (flexibility)	State-owned CFs	Private CFs
Permanent employees and fixed wage costs (no flexibility)	Private CFs	

with the clients are bound to these professionals (see Chapter 2), the ability to recruit, hire or have the exclusive right to qualified professionals will be a crucial competitive factor for the CFs.

In Table 7.4, I show the different employment strategies that private and state-owned CFs can choose from these two starting points. The private CFs must choose between the lower left corner, where they have the exclusive right to their permanent employees but pay full-time wages, have costs for offices and a low flexibility, and the upper right corner, where they temporarily hire professionals and have high flexibility, but must compete for the professionals with other firms and may experience problems in hiring qualified professionals. A third alternative for the private CFs is, of course, a combination of these two alternatives, where some professionals are temporarily hired and others are permanently employed. In contrast, the Swed-firms, which have few permanent employees, can hire professionals from their parent operators and have the exclusive right to do so, meaning that no private CF is allowed to hire professionals from these operators. The Swed-firms are therefore placed in the upper left corner, where they have the exclusive right to the professionals in their parent companies at the same time as they have full flexibility. Exclusive right for the state-owned CF does not mean that it can hire whichever professional it would like in the parent operator, but rather that only the Swed-firm and no private CF can hire these professionals. If the parent operator refuses to hire out a specific professional to the Swed-firm, there are many other similar professionals who can be hired out (though not all of them are highly qualified). If these rules apply and the Swed-firm does not pay an extra fee to the parent operator for the increased flexibility and the exclusive right to the pool of professionals, then there is no doubt that the Swed-firms enjoy a competitive advantage compared with the private CFs.[7]

---

[7] Many key persons in private CFs, which I have interviewed, claim that the Swed-firms exploit unfair competitive advantages compared with the private CFs. Here, I not only mention three of their arguments, but also why they are not valid. *Argument A*: The Swed-firms have few permanent employees and instead hire professionals. Thereby, they have low fixed costs for offices

In practice, when the Swed-firms hire professionals from their parent companies, these professionals take leave and the Swed-firms only pay salaries, subsistence levels and other project-specific costs for the temporarily hired professionals. The Swed-firms pay nothing extra, however, for their privileged position.[8] When private CFs hire professionals in the free market, these professionals also take a leave.[9] Thus, the private CFs have similar costs as the Swed-firms when hiring professionals temporarily, but have higher search costs and a higher probability that there will be restrictions on the production if they do not find any professionals to hire. The Swed-firms thus have a competitive advantage compared with the private CFs.

The fact is that the state-owned parent companies of the Swed-firms could be placed in the lower right corner of Table 7.4. The operators will take responsibility for their permanent employees when the Swed-firms do not wish to hire them. This means that if one considers a Swed-firm and its parent company as *one* firm, this fictitious firm has no advantages in the hiring of, and

---

and pay only for the personnel as long as the contract lasts. In contrast, almost all private CFs have permanent employees, meaning that the costs for offices are higher and the firms have to pay salaries whether the firms have tasks for their employees or not. This argument is not valid, because private CFs do not need to have permanent employees. The private CFs can also hire professionals on a project basis. *Argument B*: The Swed-firms have exclusive rights to the professionals employed in their parent companies. Private CFs may not hire professionals from the state-owned operators and have therefore a competitive disadvantage. This argument is also invalid. The private CFs have exclusive rights to the permanent employees in their own companies. If they wish to use a professional employed by a state-owned operator, they can always offer this professional a permanent position. *Argument C*: Taxpayers' money should not be used to finance state-owned firms that compete with private firms. Such tax-financed firms do not demand the same rate of return as private CFs, and can thereby charge a lower fee for a given quantity and quality of services. A counter-argument is that many parent companies of the Swed-firms (e.g., Vattenfall, Telia, SJ) are not financed through taxes, but run business in a similar, albeit not identical, way to private firms. However, it is not clear whether these operators are subjected to the same profit constraints as that of private firms. Other state-owned operators are financed through taxes (e.g., the Swedish National Road Administration). The argument may therefore only be valid in some cases. But then it is also necessary to prove that such state-owned CFs do charge a lower fee than do private CFs. In principle, Arguments A and B must be combined as in Table 7.4 to show that the Swed-firms do have a privileged position.

[8] Swedavia seems to be the only exception among the Swed-firms to pay hiring fees that are close to market fees. In addition to paying salaries and subsistence levels, they also pay for overhead costs and a small profit to the parent operator. It is not clear, however, whether these extra fees are based on market prices or not. Furthermore, SwedeRail pays some overhead costs to the parent operator when the professionals are hired on short-term contracts, but not for long-term contracts. Another Swed-firm, which is not included in the sample, Swedesurvey, has the same conditions as SwedeRail when hiring professionals from its parent company.

[9] The professionals in "the free market" are mostly permanently employed in the government administration or in private firms, either in the domestic market or abroad. They usually take leave when hired by the private CFs.

exclusive right to, professionals compared with private firms. The fictitious firm would have the same problems as the private CFs in finding full-time tasks for its permanent employees. Thus, the losses to the parent operator in terms of flexibility and exclusive rights will exactly offset the gains to the Swed-firm. The problem is that the parent operator—which obviously sacrifices some resources for its Swed-firm—operates in another sector from that of the Swed-firm and the private CFs. The state-owned operators in Sweden operate in partly regulated markets, often have a market position that is close to a monopoly, and have no or few requirement for profit maximization. They can therefore afford to lose some flexibility or resources. The flexibility and exclusive rights trans-ferred to the Swed-firm could, however, be decisive in the consulting sector. The competition in the consulting sector is distorted, which is disadvantageous for the private CFs. In other words, the state-owned operators *cross-subsidize* their affiliated Swed-firms. The point is that even if the Swed-firm has to pay the same fee to the state-owned operator for hiring professionals as a private CF does to pay for hiring professionals in the free market, the Swed-firm is subsidized anyway. The Swed-firm can always be sure to hire professionals, but a private CF with a hiring strategy always faces the risk of not finding a pro-fessional who can execute the project. This means that the private CF will have higher search costs for professionals and larger restrictions on its production of services.

7.4 Predation by Putting Rivals at a Cost Disadvantage

Now we turn to the question of whether or not the privileged position of the Swed-firms is unfair. The problem with unfair competitive advantages in the Swedish consulting sector is similar to an example of what is called "predation by putting rivals at a cost disadvantage" in the Industrial Organization literature (Ordover and Saloner, 1989).[10] As shown in Figure 7.6, a downstream firm (state-owned CF) signs an exclusive dealing contract with an upstream firm (infrastructure operator), which is the dominating supplier of intermediates (professionals) in the market. This operator agrees to supply professionals only to the state-owned CF and not to the rival firm (private CF). Alternatively, the operator hires out professionals to the private CF, but only on unfavorable terms; for example, the private CF is forced to hire professionals via the Swed-firm, thereby raising the hiring costs, or the private CF must offer the professionals a permanent position but then loses flexibility (see Table 7.4).

---

[10] The term predation (from predatory) means here anticompetitive business strategies that have the effect of lowering a properly evaluated, measured social welfare.

Figure 7.6. The relationship between state-owned operators and CFs.

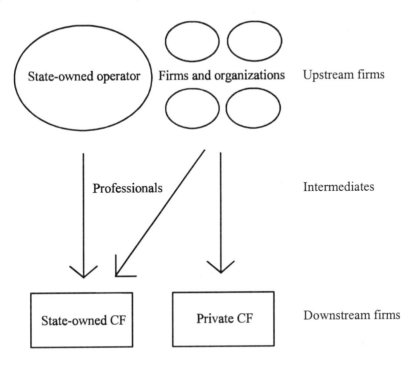

According to Ordover and Saloner (1989), three conditions must be fulfilled to motivate the two parties in such an exclusive dealing contract: 1) The private CF must be hurt in terms of profit by the contract; 2) The private CF should not be able to respond to the state-owned CF's exclusive contract, for example, by making a similar deal with the other suppliers of professionals in the market; and 3) The state-owned operator's profit must be raised by the exclusive contract, compared with that seen if the operator chooses to hire out professionals to any CF.

Clearly, the private CF's profit is negatively affected by the exclusive dealing contract, because the costs of searching for professionals to hire are raised, and production restraints are imposed as the probability increases that the private CF will find no professionals to hire. Thus, the state-owned CF's actions raise the costs at which the rival can obtain professionals.[11] Furthermore, the private CF likely cannot respond to the exclusion by making a deal with other suppliers of professionals, because the other suppliers are small and scattered, and, as I discuss next, it is doubtful that the other suppliers will profit from such

---

[11] Some of the private CFs will then be forced out of business in the international market. In fact, this has already occurred in Sweden.

a deal. Furthermore, the state-owned CF is not limited to hiring professionals from its parent operator, but can also hire professionals in the free market and compete with the private CF for the few remaining professionals who are still available for hire in the market. Thus, the first and second conditions are fulfilled.

However, the parent operator likely will not increase its profit by signing an exclusive contract with an affiliated Swed-firm. It would be more profitable for the operator to let any of the CFs hire professionals. Put another way, would a private operator own, and cross-subsidize, an affiliated private CF? As was argued in Chapter 2, the reason the CFs are separated from the operators is that the operators cannot employ professionals who supply specialized services full-time. At the same time, these professionals have alternative tasks for other operators. The professionals are therefore organized in separate firms, that is, in CFs. The Swedish state-owned operators do not have full-time occupation for some of their professionals. Therefore, these professionals are hired out to other operators abroad, and the foreign operations are organized in Swed-firms. If the professionals are not employed full-time, then the operator must take the loss, one that a private profit-maximizing operator would never accept. From a profit maximization point of view, the existence of Swed-firms is, in other words, a token of government inefficiency. The state-owned operator's choice not to maximize profits is likely to stem from the fact that the owner, the government, has other goals to prioritize than to maximize the value of its firms. For example, a political goal may be to keep the unemployment rate at a low level. The government may then refuse to allow the state-owned operators to lay off personnel for whom they have no full-time tasks. Under these conditions, it can be an optimal strategy for the state-owned operator to keep professionals in-house by offering them permanent employment and letting them, for example, consult in foreign markets when they are not needed in the daily production. However, when there are no tasks for them, the state-owned operator must accept the costs. Under such a government employment restriction, the third condition for motivating the exclusive dealing contract is fulfilled.

It is improbable that the combination of an operator and a CF in one firm, or an exclusive dealing contract between them, would create any synergy effects or that it would be a superior way to organize production. *These arguments are strengthened by the fact that the private operators in the infrastructure sectors in Sweden or in any other developed country seldom have their own consulting affiliates or underused professionals in-house.* The few cases when private operators do have their own affiliated CFs occur when the private operators have recently become market oriented. After some years, the affiliated CFs are separated. If the combined operator-CF were a superior way to organize production, there should exist many such combined operator-CFs in the private sector. However, there are not. This indicates that there are no synergies.[12] The conclusions are that the cross-subsidy must be unfair because a private CF would never be able to gain such an advantage in a competitive market, and that, under profit-maximization, the third condition for putting rival firms at a disadvantage is not fulfilled. Thus, it would be more profitable for the operator to let *any* CF hire professionals. The preceding reasoning also explains why it is so difficult for the private CFs to make an exclusive deal with other profit-maximizing suppliers of professionals in the market.

The parent operator may have two purposes for hiring out its employees to CFs, which in turn implement projects for other operators abroad: 1) The parent operator will gain flexibility in its operation, because it does not need to pay salaries to employees who are hired out if the operator faces overcapacity; and 2) The competence and experience of the employees will be upgraded as these employees face new problems to solve in international projects. To obtain these goals, however, it is not necessary for the operator to own an affiliated CF. The first goal can be obtained if the affiliated state-owned CF is separated from the operator and this CF thereby offers some of the professionals employed by the operator a permanent position. The separated CF can then hire out its professionals on a project basis to the former parent operator and to operators abroad. The first goal can also be obtained if several CFs are allowed to temporarily hire professionals from the operator in a competitive way. It is then likely that the operator can be better paid for the professionals it hires out than if there is only one affiliated CF that has the exclusive right to hire professionals. If the operator wishes to obtain the second goal and keep professionals with upgraded competence in-house, then it would also be an appropriate strategy to let several CFs hire professionals on a project basis from the operator. This strategy would be, for the operator, at least as good as owning an affiliated CF.

Today, there is a debate in Sweden about whether many of the large state-owned operators in the infrastructure sectors should be privatized. Some of these operators formerly had a monopoly in the Swedish market (e.g., Telia, Vattenfall, SJ), but market deregulations were introduced in recent years that allowed competing private operators to exist today.[13] One can expect that as state-owned operators in Sweden become more market oriented, their affiliates, that is, the Swed-firms, will be sold off and organized in separate firms. When the operators become privately owned and face profit maximization requirements, they will clearly not accept being placed in the lower right corner of

---

[12] In fact, the scientific burden of proof rests with the person or firm who claims that there are synergies, not with the person who believes that there are no synergies, or cannot find any.

[13] Other government authorities, like the Swedish National Road Administration, the Swedish Civil Aviation Administration and the National Land Survey of Sweden, still face a monopoly position and use affiliated Swed-firms in overseas operations.

Table 7.4 and cross-subsidizing the Swed-firms. The Swed-firms will then lose the competitive advantage they have today compared with the private CFs.[14] Recently, privatizations of state-owned CFs have occurred. Swedec and SGAB, two CFs that specialize in educational systems and geology, were formerly state-owned CFs, but were acquired by Hifab in 1988 and 1992, respectively. SwedPlan was recently sold off to a foundation. In the mid-1990s, the state-owned forest administrator Domänverket was privatized at the same time as it merged the pulp and paper firm Assi and founded AssiDomän. Swedforest, an affiliated state-owned CF to Domänverket, was then separated and later acquired by SCC. When a Swed-firm is separated from its parent operator, it can either choose a strategy with permanent employees or continue to hire professionals from its ex-parent, but now in competition with other private CFs. A third alternative is to merge with a private CF, as Swedforest did.

7.5 Consequences of the Exclusive Dealing Contract

Apart from private Swedish CFs suffering from unfair competition, there are two main implications of the exclusive dealing contracts between the Swed-firms and their parent operators, irrespective of whether or not these contracts are motivated. First, the market for management professionals in Sweden is blocked and thereby a desired restructuring of the whole Swedish consulting sector is prevented. It has therefore been difficult for the Swedish private CFs to adapt themselves to the market trends and to choose any of the three strategies mentioned in Section 7.2. The private CFs in other European countries have not faced such a blockade to the same extent in their domestic markets and so have been able to restructure and upgrade their management skills through either employing management professionals permanently or hiring them temporarily. The Swedish blockade has taken the attitude that it is almost impossible for a private CF to find management professionals to hire in the domestic market. Many of the private CFs have therefore been forced to hire foreign professionals.

Second, Sida is another large loser on the blockade caused by the exclusive dealing contracts. In recent years, Sida has had problems with motivating CFs to submit proposals when management services have been procured. Mostly, there are only three tenderers, or sometimes even two tenderers (although five or six are invited) that submit proposals (Sida, 1999b). It is likely that the

---

[14] To be fair, it should also be mentioned that the tendency for Swed-firms to be more interested in project-wise associations with the most internationalized private Swedish CFs has been recognized in recent years. Market experience and complementary services can then be combined.

existence of state-owned CFs has meant that the competition level among the tenderers has been lower compared with what it would have been in a free consulting market, where any private CF could hire professionals from the state-owned infrastructure operators. A consequence of the limited competition and the fact that few CFs submit proposals when Sida procures consulting services is that Sida has started to invite foreign CFs to participate in the tenders. At the same time, Swedish CFs are not allowed to tender for projects financed by foreign bilateral development agencies (see discussion in section 4.2). I argue that the limited competition in Sweden is the main reason that Sida invites foreign CFs and not because Sida wishes to have a less protectionistic policy than its corresponding agencies in other developed countries.

The problem with cross-subsidized Swedish state-owned CFs also concerns foreign private CFs when they compete with the Swed-firms for projects financed by multilateral development agencies or commercial projects. The foreign private CFs have a disadvantage compared with the cross-subsidized Swed-firms, but are not as hurt as the Swedish private CFs, because their domestic market is not blocked and they can freely hire professionals in their domestic markets. Of course, Swedish private CFs can reduce the damage by hiring professionals in other countries, but they still have a disadvantage compared with the state-owned CFs because of the subsidies. Finally, the phenomenon with state-owned CFs is not limited to Sweden. Other countries have also state-owned or semi-state-owned CFs that possess unfair competitive advantages—but not to the same extent as in Sweden.

7.6 Summary

During the last decade, the composition of services demanded in international projects has changed, especially when development agencies are involved. Engineering services are to a higher degree procured from local TCFs. At the same time, management services are more frequently included in the projects and procured from international CFs. The engineering services that are still purchased from the latter CFs aim more to facilitate knowledge transfer to the host country. This trend stems from local TCFs having learned to replicate engineering services as a consequence of more training from, and cooperation with, international CFs. Moreover, the trend toward privatizations and market deregulations in the infrastructure sectors also explains the shift to management services. As local CFs learn how to replicate management services implemented by international CFs, one can expect that the trend toward new services will continue and that the latter CFs will be forced to supply even more sophisticated services in the future.

There are several consequences of this trend for the international CFs. First, they have to acquire new kinds of skills and to recruit personnel who can supply management services. Second, cooperation with inexpensive local TCFs that can provide bulk design services will increase in importance. Third, management services mainly take the form of labor services when compared with design services, which mostly are supplied in document form. A larger part of the time will be spent in the host country when supplying management services. Thus, costs for reimbursements will be higher, but costs for offices at home will be lower. Fourth, the fact that contacts and cooperation with the client will be more frequent implies that social competence of the professionals and good communication with the clients will become more important. Fifth, more labor services means that knowledge transfer should be intensified. Sixth, fewer engineering services implies that the interdependence between TCFs and contractors that originate in developed countries will become weaker in the international market.

In Sweden, private CFs have problems in recruiting management professionals; these problems are closely related to the presence of state-owned CFs. The latter CFs are affiliates of government infrastructure operators that have a large number of management professionals in-house. It can be argued that the Swed-firms enjoy an unfair competitive advantage compared with the private CFs. In principle, a private CF can choose between two employment strategies: 1) to have permanent employees, fixed wage costs and exclusive rights to these employees; or 2) to hire professionals on a project basis when contracts are awarded. The CF will then have flexible wage costs but no exclusive rights to the hired professionals. A Swed-firm, on the other hand, can hire professionals from its parent company with exclusive rights; that is, no private CF is allowed to hire these professionals. Thus, the Swed-firm has both exclusive right *and* full flexibility. Since the Swed-firms do not pay extra for the privilege, they are cross-subsidized by their parent operators. This kind of privileged position is called "predation by putting rivals at a cost disadvantage", and will cause the private CFs to have higher costs when searching for professionals to hire and larger restrictions on their production of services. It is not likely that the combination of an operator and a CF in one firm is an effective way to organize the production, because similar combined firms are rarely observed in the private sector. It is rather a sign of government inefficiency of the operator. Since the Swed-firms in principle blockade the Swedish infrastructure market for management professionals, they prevent a necessary restructuring of the consulting sector. It is also likely that the existence of these CFs will decrease rather than increase the competition in the consulting market, particularly when Sida procures consulting services. The problems could easily be solved by allowing *any* CF to hire professionals from the operators. The operators would then probably earn a higher profit.

Chapter 8

SUCCESS STRATEGIES AND COMPETITIVENESS IN THE GLOBAL MARKET

In this chapter, various strategies and competitiveness by consulting firms (CFs) in the international market are examined. First, I analyze the strategy of focusing on specific host countries and setting up representative offices. Second, I consider various strategies: the choice between having permanent employees and hiring professionals on a project basis, whether it is optimal to tender only for large contracts with high expected profitability, and so on. In addition to finding strategies that have been successful, strategies that have been less successful are also considered. I then analyze whether it is advisable to co-operate with and follow contractors and investment material suppliers when going abroad. Furthermore, the role of government authorities that subsidize consulting exports is analyzed, as well as the performance by Swedish CFs in a market financed by multilateral development agencies.

8.1 Focus on Specific Host Countries

In this section, the issues of why and whether CFs focus on specific host countries and establish representative offices are examined. As mentioned in Chapter 3, when export contracts occur more frequently in a host country, representative offices can be established as a support for the export strategy to create networks with decision makers, develop long-term relationships with old and potential clients, and source information about potential projects and conditions in the host country. As concluded in Chapter 6, a representative office increases the probability that the CF will 1) be invited to tender for projects taking place in the host country; and 2) win tenders when proposals are submitted. A representative office will not yield any direct incomes and can be seen as a host country-specific fixed cost. The CF must therefore have a large sales volume in that host country to afford such an office. Preferably, there should be more than one potential client for the CF in that host country, but the local demand for the CF's services does not need to be continuous as in the case of permanent offices. Furthermore, in recent years when clients have had more to say about the selection of the CF, it has become more important for the CF to be represented in the local market to maintain contact with previous, and potential, local clients.

An appropriate and perhaps profitable strategy could be to focus the export efforts on specific countries where the firm can get a foothold and establish representative offices, which in turn increases the probability of being invited to submit tenders and of winning them. Among the firms in the sample, this strategy has successfully been applied by Hifab International and SWECO and partly by SwedPower and Swedtel. As described in Table 3.3, 34 Swedish representative offices are established in emerging markets, primarily by the four aforementioned CFs. Also, previous experience with the host country will, as concluded in Chapter 6, increase the probability of being invited for more tenders in that country, but will not increase the probability of winning a tender if the firm has been invited. As was shown in Table 4.1, a Sida-financed contract is probably the easiest way to gain experience with a new host country. When the CF tries to get a contract for a new client in a country with which the CF already has experience, Table 4.2 indicates that Sida is also likely to be the financier of that contract. The value of old reference assignments in a host country or for a client will deteriorate over time. By focusing the export efforts on selected host countries or regions, the CF can refresh the reference list at a lower cost than if the CF tries to win contracts in new countries and for new clients.[1]

Table 8.1 shows the extent to which the Swedish CFs in the sample submit proposals to, and win contracts in, host countries where a local office is established compared with countries where no local office is set up. The table indicates that 458 proposals were submitted to 318 different host countries; that is, on average, each of the 31 CFs in the sample submitted 15 proposals to 10 different host countries. On average, around 2.0 proposals were submitted to each host country where a representative office is established and 1.75 proposals to countries where a permanent office is established, compared with 1.36 proposals to host countries with no local office.[2] A similar relation between these three groups can be found for the average number of awarded contracts (1.10, 1.17 and 0.65, respectively), but the averages are lower, of course, because many tenders are lost in competition.

When considering Table 8.1, one should remember that the average number of proposals and awarded contracts in the three groups of host countries are only what is *observed* in the sample. Since the CFs submit no proposals at all to most host countries where no local offices are established, the actual average number of proposals submitted to, and contracts awarded in, such host countries is

---

[1] However, the sales of services to a client should not be too continuous, particularly not if commercial projects are involved, because then it may be more profitable for the client to employ the professionals directly.

[2] The 458 proposals are only a sample of all proposals submitted abroad between 1995 and 1997. The actual average number of proposals per host country is therefore considerably higher (three to five times higher) for all three groups of host countries.

Table 8.1. Proposals submitted to, and awarded contracts in, host countries in which Swedish CFs have a representative, a permanent or no office between 1995 and 1997 in number and average number.

The CF has a local office in the host country	Number of host countries (Note! Combinations of CFs and host countries)		Proposals			Awarded contracts		
	(A) In sample	(B) Total	Total number	Average number per host country		Total number	Average number per host country	
				(A) In sample	(B) Total		(A) In sample	(B) Total
No office	277	1,500	378	1.36	0.25	181	0.65	0.12
Representative office	29	34	59	2.03	1.74	32	1.10	0.94
Permanent office	12	36	21	1.75	0.58	14	1.17	0.39
Total	318	1,570	458	1.44	0.29	227	0.71	0.14

Note: The thirty-one CFs in the sample have submitted 458 proposals to 318 host countries (= number of combinations of firms *and* host countries in the sample). On average, each firm has thus submitted proposals to 10 different host countries. However, there are more combinations of CFs and host countries because these CFs have submitted no proposals at all to most of the host countries. According to Table 3.4, Swedish CFs (including NCG in Table 3.4) have representative offices in 34 host countries and permanent offices in 36 host countries. The total number of relevant combinations of CFs and host countries where no local office is established can be estimated to at least 1500 (31 firms times 50 host countries). The 458 submitted proposals are only a sample of proposals submitted abroad. Thereby, the actual number of proposals submitted to, and number of awarded contracts awarded in, the three groups of host countries (no office, representative office and permanent office) should be considerably higher (3-5 times higher) between 1995 and 1997.

considerably lower than 1.36 and 0.65, respectively. Let us say that there are 1,500 such relevant host countries (e.g., 31 firms times 50 host countries); then the average number of proposals and contracts should be 0.25 and 0.12, respectively. On the other hand, the actual number of host countries where the CFs have a representative office is 34 (instead of 29), and there are 36 (instead of 12) host countries where a permanent office is established.[3] It is obvious that the highest average number of submitted proposals and awarded contracts (1.74 and 0.94, respectively) can be found in host countries with a representative office. The average number of proposals submitted to, and contracts awarded in, host countries with a permanent local office is considerably lower at 0.58 and 0.39, respectively, but still higher than in host countries where no office is set up. The large difference between host countries with representative and permanent offices is explained by the fact that most of the permanent offices are established in developed countries and are not coordinated with exports form Sweden. On the other hand, the aim of a representative office is almost always to promote exports from the home country. Thus, the CFs seem primarily to focus their export efforts on host countries where representative offices have been set up and on emerging markets where permanent offices are established.

In Table 8.2, host countries with which CFs have previous experience and those with which they have no such experience are similarly analyzed. On average, the CFs have submitted 1.52 proposals to, and been awarded 0.79 contracts in, host countries with which they have previous experience, compared with 1.13 proposals to, and 0.48 contracts in, host countries where they have no experience. Thus, the CFs seem to focus on specific host countries with which they have previous experience. Once again, only a sample of host countries where the CFs have submitted at least one proposal is considered. There are many other countries to which the firms have not submitted any proposals at all, primarily where the CFs have no previous contracts. Thus, if all countries were considered, the differences would be even larger for the average number of proposals and awarded contracts than that shown in the table. As many as 337, or 74%, of the 458 proposals are submitted to host countries where the CFs have previous experience. On the other hand, the CFs in the sample have previous experience with, on average, only 30% to 40% of all potential markets.

---

[3] See Table 3.3, where there are 34 representative offices and 36 permanent offices (either majority or minority owned) if one also takes into account NCG's foreign offices in Table 3.4.

Table 8.2. Proposals submitted to, and awarded contracts in, host countries with which Swedish CFs have and have not previous experience between 1995 and 1997 in number and average number.

The CF has previous experience with the host country	Number of host countries (Note! combinations of CFs and host countries in the sample where the CFs have submitted proposals)	Proposals		Awarded contracts	
		Total number	Average number per host country	Total number	Average number per host country
No	107	121	1.13	51	0.48
Yes	222	337	1.52	176	0.79
All	318	458	1.44	227	0.71

Note: For the number of host countries (n=318) see comments to Table 8.1. In 11 cases, a CF has submitted a proposal to a new host country and won the contract, *and*, thereafter, this CF has submitted further proposals to that host country. Therefore, the sum of the number of combinations for the "no" and "yes" groups is 329 instead of 318. The 458 submitted proposals are only a sample of proposals submitted abroad. Thereby, the actual number of proposals submitted to, and awarded in, host countries with which the tenderer has previous experience and no such experience should be considerably higher (3-5 times higher) between 1995 and 1997.

8.2 The Modern Consulting Firm

In this section, I discuss successful strategies in the international market by presenting some of the Swedish CFs in the sample. To begin with, Hifab International is today the most successful Swedish CF in the market to be financed by multilateral development agencies, partly because this firm has applied strategies that have resulted in maximum flexibility. In the international market, Hifab International supplies both technical support and management services, and not technical design services, because competition from local technical consulting firms (TCFs) has meant that the pressure on fee levels for such services has increased (see Section 7.1).[4] When design services are needed in a project, Hifab International creates a temporary joint venture with a TCF from a developed country or from the host country where the project is implemented. Thus, Hifab is a typical modern CF that has chosen a multidisciplinary strategy, as mentioned in Section 7.2 (strategy 2). Hifab International has systematically developed a marketing program that is geared toward the multilateral development agencies (when these agencies are susceptible for such marketing) and has, for example, together with eight other European CFs, invested in a small firm that specializes in procurement and tender procedures of the EU funds. When tendering for projects financed by multilateral development agencies, Hifab International has strived to win a large number of contracts for each multilateral development agency, so that fixed costs associated with each agency can be spread across a large sales volume. Hifab International seems to be the CF in the sample that has invested most in learning the tender rules of these agencies.

As was discussed in Section 7.3, a private CF can either choose to have permanent employees and take full responsibility for their salaries, or hire professionals temporarily on a project basis in competition with other firms. Hifab International applies a variant of the second employment strategy—called the Shamrock model—to achieve optimal flexibility, thereby differing from most other private Swedish CFs in the sample. Administrative personnel at the head office and strategic professionals with important long-term relationships with clients, who stand for the continuity and culture of the firm, are permanently employed, whereas the rest of the professionals are hired on long-term (more than one year) or short-term (months up to one year) contracts. The professionals are hired either in Sweden, in other developed countries or in the local

---

[4] In the domestic market, Hifab is a typical project management CF that supplies technical support services and has dropped technical design services. Hifab International has been successful in transforming the firm's project management skills, which were learned when implementing investment projects, into management skills that are necessary during restructuring.

market where the project takes place. In practice, this means that only 20% to 30% of the field-posted professionals are permanently employed at Hifab International.

An obvious advantage with hiring professionals temporarily is, of course, that the CF will not need to pay salaries to employees when the firm has no contracts for them. The firm can more easily adjust the pool of professionals to the level of demand and number of contracts, thereby avoiding over- and under-capacity to a higher degree and incurring lower office costs compared with CFs that hire permanent employees. As mentioned in the previous chapter, management services are to a larger extent supplied as labor at the site of the client. It would then be a waste of resources to have an office at home for those professionals supplying such services. In other words, supplying technical support and management services and applying a strategy with temporarily hired professionals should be an effective combination.

Perhaps the largest advantage with this hiring strategy is that the CF can more easily adapt the skills and experiences of the professionals to new trends in demand from the consulting market. If new skills and experiences are demanded, then the firm can simply try to find and to hire new kinds of professionals who match this demand. Such a shift has been a reality in recent years when management skills have been more in demand (see Chapter 7). Not surprisingly, Hifab International is the private Swedish CF that has adjusted itself best to this trend. Most of the other private Swedish CFs that specialize in design services and have permanent employees have practically been pinioned by the strict Swedish employment laws. Hifab International's flexible employment strategy implies that this firm—like a chameleon—can take on several forms and dimensions within a short period of time and can supply a wide range of engineering and management services in miscellaneous sectors like transport infrastructure, environment, housing, social infrastructure and government administration.

Hiring professionals on a project basis is, however, sometimes a problematic strategy. The professionals must be hired in competitive market conditions with other CFs. Such professionals are sometimes permanently employed in public administration or in larger private firms, implying that they must take a leave to work on contract. The hiring process is made even more complicated by the fact that the CF does not know whether the contract will be awarded or not when the CF first asks the professional if he or she is interested in participating in the project. The CF will often have to overbook a specific professional in several tender documents. The risk is then that the CF may win a contract but will have no professionals to implement the project. The problem with undercapacity is also valid for CFs that apply the strategy of having permanent employees. On the other hand, the overcapacity problem will only be suffered by CFs that have permanent employees. In Sweden there will be particular problems in hiring professionals temporarily because a significant part of the market is blocked by the state-owned CFs (see Chapter 7). In spite of this blockade, Hifab International has managed to find loopholes to hire professionals on a project basis anyway. It is not surprising that many professionals are hired outside Sweden (around 30% to 40%). A hiring strategy requires a large network between the managers in the CF and the professionals employed in other firms and authorities. Logistics will be an important problem to solve.

Other problems may also arise with temporarily hired professionals. Such professionals have fewer incentives to stand for the brand name of the CF and may take less responsibility for the project if they have no long-term commitments with the CF. To avoid this situation, the CF can use the strategy of hiring the same professionals on a regular basis. The accumulation and sharing of knowledge within the firm likely will be less if the CF applies a hiring strategy. Hired professionals stationed in different countries rarely meet each other because they only have a contract for the CF as long as the project lasts. Much of the knowledge that the temporarily hired professionals learn when executing services in new environments will therefore not be assimilated by the CF or the permanently employed professionals. The temporarily hired professionals will instead bring the new experience and knowledge with them to their permanent employers, who may assimilate this knowledge.[5] A CF that applies a hiring strategy must therefore be an expert on identifying knowledge, and will partly let other firms and authorities (the hired professionals' permanent employers) take responsibility for the knowledge accumulation and sharing.

It is not necessary to be as extreme as Hifab International and only have 20% of the field-posted professionals permanently employed to obtain flexibility. A strategy with 70% to 80% of the professionals permanently employed and the rest hired on a project basis would be a step in the right direction that would increase the flexibility of the CF considerably. The strict regulations in the Swedish labor market, however, where it is almost impossible to fire permanent employees, make it difficult to change from a permanent strategy to a hiring strategy. If the CF prefers a hiring strategy, then this option should have been chosen from the beginning.

An alternative way for a more traditional TCF to upgrade the competence of management skills is to merge with a management consulting firm (MCF). A merger in the consulting sector is expected to be particularly successful if the CFs have complementary supplied services that can be sold to the same clients.

---

[5] If a CF with a hiring strategy wishes to accumulate and later diffuse the newly acquired knowledge within the firm, then the core staff must travel extensively to coordinate the operations, an action that will be very expensive if the CF is operating abroad.

The firms need not actually have the same clients before the merger; the point is that they will have a strong advantage if they could have had the same clients. Scope economies (diversifying advantages) can then be fully used, because client- and project-specific fixed costs—such as information and contract costs, as well as fixed costs to create confidence for, and long-term relationships with, a client—can be spread across a larger sales volume to that client or project. The MCF division will then be able to sell complementing management services to the TCF's clients, and the TCF division can sell complementing engineering services to the MCF's clients. As a response to the trend toward management services in the international market, the Swedish firms ÅF and ISO Swedish Management Group merged in early 1998. The former CF has by tradition based its operations on engineering services, whereas the latter firm supplies only management services. From a theoretical point of view, this is one of the most promising reconfigurations in the Swedish consulting sector in several years. Much work must be done, however, before the firms can be fully integrated. It is worth mentioning that ISO also has applied a hiring strategy of professionals like that of Hifab International.

Instead of focusing on management services, a strategy with spearhead technology in selected areas of the market is possible (strategy 1 in Section 7.2). This strategy requires a continuous upgrading of the engineering services and the knowledge base to stay at least one step ahead of local TCFs. SWECO and ÅF are two traditional TCFs that have applied this strategy, but they also have elements of management services in their projects.[6] SWECO specializes in engineering services in the energy, water and environment sectors, and, apart from supplying management services via the ISO division in multiple sectors, ÅF focuses on the energy, environment, and paper and pulp sectors. Further-more, ÅF is the firm in the sample that has gone furthest in trying to upgrade the complexity level of its engineering services with the help of information techno-logy services.

Both SWECO and ÅF each have a special division, SWECO International and ÅF International, with only two to three employees who are contract parties to the clients/financiers. However, the projects are implemented by SWECO's and ÅF's usual divisions. Through their International divisions, SWECO and ÅF coordinate their foreign operations, where much of their knowledge about the procurement rules for different development agencies has accumulated. SWECO has applied this strategy since the 1960s, whereas ÅF introduced it in 1997. SWECO International also markets the other SWECO divisions abroad, guaran-tees the quality of executed services and projects, confers with the other divi-

---

[6] Whereas ÅF has chosen to cooperate continuously with ISO Swedish Management Group through a merger, SWECO cooperates with different MCFs on a project basis.

sions about advisable CFs to cooperate with, studies international market trends, and, on that basis, selects strategies. Furthermore, SWECO founded a new division in 1997, SWECO Project Management, which specializes in project management services. This affiliate is likely to be used in foreign markets.

Swedtel is the only Swedish CF that is a world market leader in the sector where it operates. Swedtel's turnover has grown by 139% between 1992 and 1996, which can be explained by the fact that this firm took the opportunity to expand when the telecom sector was deregulated and telecom operators were privatized worldwide. This means that countries that formerly had only one telecom operator (client) now have two to four operators. The high growth in mobile telecom meant large investments in new systems, which in turn increased the demand for consulting services. In emerging markets, the telecom operators work to a higher degree on a commercial basis and have substantially higher purchasing power than do other government clients/operators in, for example, the energy, water and transport infrastructure sectors. All of these factors imply a relatively continuous and stable demand for telecom services in emerging markets. At the same time, the local competition in this sector is weak, which has made establishment of greenfield offices possible in these regions (see Table 3.1). Like the other state-owned CFs, Swedtel has successfully applied a strategy with temporarily hired professionals and focuses more on supplying management services than do private CFs. However, Swedtel has had assistance from its parent operator (Telia) in two senses. First, as was analyzed in Chapter 7, Swedtel and most of the other state-owned CFs have an unfair competitive advantage compared with private CFs because they can hire professionals from their parent operators and no other CFs are allowed to do this. Second, around one-third of Swedtel's export is internal export to Telia's majority-owned foreign affiliates abroad. Of the other two-thirds, some exports are directed to minority-owned foreign affiliates of Telia, but this amount is unknown.

Finally, Swedavia—a state-owned CF that focuses on management services in aviation—seems to be the CF, together with Hifab International, that has gone the furthest in its lobbying and marketing ambitions directed at multilateral development agencies. For example, Swedavia established a representative office in the Philippines that can be used for marketing purposes aimed at both AsDB (whose head office is located in Manila) and potential clients in the Philippines. As was mentioned in Section 4.3, AsDB and the EU funds seem to be those development agencies that are most susceptible to marketing from the CFs. Not surprisingly, these development agencies also do a lot of the short-listing and tender evaluation themselves and allow the client minimum influence on the selection process. In fact, it is almost necessary to lobby the AsDB and EU funds to be awarded contracts on a regular basis financed by these development agencies.

8.3 Typical Mistakes

International consulting requires continuity. Using export projects as a way of smoothing fluctuations in the business cycle in the domestic market is not recommended. Many Swedish CFs that operated in the Middle East in the early 1980s (e.g., Tyréns and Rejlers) returned home when the domestic market boomed in the mid- and late 1980s. When recession arose in the domestic market in the early 1990s, many of these CFs tried to go abroad again. These efforts were, however, too late. Since the value of reference assignments deteriorate over time, the 10-year-old international reference assignments had little or no value, meaning that these firms were seldom even invited or short-listed to tender. As a consequence, these CFs had to fire many of their employees. In contrast, SWECO is the CF in the Swedish sample that has the longest continuous experience with foreign operations, and, not surprisingly, it is also the private CF that has the widest market coverage abroad.

A typical error is to tender for projects only with large contract values. Although these projects are the most profitable because scope economies can be used to a large degree, this is not a recommended strategy. The strategy will only be effective if the tenderer has had previous experience with the client. It is important to implement small projects as well, with a contract value of less than 0.3 MSEK, for example, which may not be profitable. These small contracts can be considered as a way of marketing and are mostly first contracts for new clients. The CF will then have experience with a new client, with which long-term relationships may develop, and will have the opportunity to show the client the skill and competence of the firm and its employees. One of the CFs in the sample (not mentioned by name) has during recent years only tendered for large projects, where the CF seldom has had previous experience with the client. Not surprisingly, the success rate has been very low. In the sample, awarded contracts in competition for previous clients have an average contract value of 5.4 MSEK, whereas awarded contracts for new clients are 3.9 MSEK in contract value. Thus, contracts for previous clients are larger than are those for new clients.

Another mistake occurs when CFs with similar skills and experiences found a consortium to unite their efforts in the international market. What happened with the Swedish consortiums that existed 10 to 15 years ago is well known: rivalry among the members caused the consortiums to break apart (see Section A.2 in Appendix A). Some Nordic TCFs—Swedish Tyréns, ÅF-Infrakonsult and Norwegian Reinersen—started cooperating in 1997 to pool their skills and experiences when operating abroad. These CFs are competitors to each other in the Nordic market, but now they try to cooperate abroad. All of these TCFs have limited experience with foreign operations and have fallen behind their more internationalized competitors in Sweden and Norway. A necessary condition for such a consortium to be successful is that the participating firms complement each other for supplied services. Unfortunately, they do not in this case.[7] It is therefore expected that this kind of cooperation will fail. The same rule of thumb that the CFs should complement each other counts when CFs from developed countries cooperate temporarily on a project basis.

A common error many CFs make when tendering for projects financed by multilateral development agencies is that they only tender for a few projects financed by a specific multilateral development agency and do not put enough effort into continuously tendering for such contracts. An endless number of CFs have been awarded no more than one or two small contracts (if any at all) by a multilateral development agency, and the success rates by project values for these firms have been very low. Such a performance is, of course, not profitable in the long run for the CFs, the reason being that each multilateral development agency has its own tendering procedures and rules that will take some time for the tenderers to learn. The learning can be seen as a fixed cost for the CF that is specific for each multilateral development agency. A necessary condition to be profitable is to spread these fixed learning costs over a large sales volume for that specific multilateral development agency.[8] This is especially important for the EU funds whose complicated tender rules are costly to learn. Either the CF has to focus heavily on projects financed by some multilateral development agencies and try to win as many tenders as possible, or the CF should refrain from participating in such tenders. Small and medium-sized CFs, which can only be awarded a few contracts during, for example, a five-year period for a specific multilateral development agency, should, in other words, refrain from tendering in the market financed by multilateral development agencies.

A frequently made mistake when tendering for projects financed by multilateral development agencies is that the tenderers put too much effort into specifications and methodology in the proposals, although the financier or client has not required such detailed specifications. Instead, the CFs should focus more on preparing the curricula vitae of the staff, composing better teams and suggesting team leaders with more merit. This is particularly important when the World Bank and the regional development banks are involved in the projects, because these development agencies seem to apply their point systems in the evaluations more strictly than do other development agencies (see Chapter 6).

Contracts financed by bilateral development agencies should be applied more to opening up new markets for the CF. Such reference assignments can be

---

[7] Key persons in the two Swedish TCFs have gone so far as to suggest that Swedish TCFs as a group should compose a national team of TCFs that would cooperate abroad.

[8] Thus, a large firm size in itself will not be a comparative advantage, but rather a large sales volume for a specific multilateral development agency will be an advantage.

used to win projects financed by multilateral development agencies or commercial projects. Although the commercial market in many sectors is still limited today because of the clients' financial situation, this market should be more important in the future. As was seen in Table 4.1, the function of bilateral development agencies as a spearhead for the CFs is in one sense to help the CFs get a contract for a new client, and only in a second sense to open up a new host country for the CFs. Many CFs do not use this opportunity—especially not the Swedish CFs, which prefer to try to win another Sida-financed contract. Multilateral development agencies often require that the CF and its staff have previous experience with the host country. Such experiences will substantially increase the probability that the CF will be short-listed. However, the probability of winning a contract financed by a multilateral development agency for a new client in an old host country is still low, as described in Table 4.2. Many CFs seem to overestimate the weight of host country experience when tendering for multilateral and commercial contracts.

A classical trap to avoid is procurement with a hidden agenda (see Chapter 6). The client has in this situation already decided from the beginning which supplier to select, but may procure a project in competition anyway—either because he or she is forced to procure in competition by the financier, or because he or she wishes to subject a previous supplier to competitive pressure. The problem for the CF is to identify such tenders before the proposal has been submitted. Tenders should be avoided when the competitors have previous contracts for the client but their own firm does not. Many CFs are naive to think that they will have a chance to win the bid when they have experience with similar projects, but no experience with the client.

8.4 Cooperation with Contractors

An alternative strategy to working alone or cooperating with other international and local CFs is for a TCF either to be a subcontractor to, or found a temporary consortium with, contractors and investment material suppliers. In a consortium, the contractor will take the responsibility for the tender document and marketing, with the result that the TCF will incur lower costs for tendering and will have a lower risk, but will also have a lower expected profit margin. If the contractor already has a contract for a client and purchases engineering services directly from TCFs, the profit margin and risk are expected to be lower for the TCFs as well, because the head contractor partly can choose between different TCFs. The disadvantage with cooperating with, and selling services to, contractors is that the credibility of the TCF as an independent firm will decrease when it, on behalf of a client, procures contractor services and supervising contractors in other projects.

Fifteen years ago, it was relatively common for Swedish TCFs to follow, or found consortiums with, large contractors in the international market, especially in large turnkey projects in the Middle East. The most famous Swedish example is perhaps SWECO, which during several decades cooperated with large contractors such as ABB and Skanska in the hydro power sector. Today, this kind of cooperation strategy is primarily chosen by specialized TCFs that either cannot supply a full range of services for a project themselves or have limited experience with foreign operations. Such TCFs can be found operating in the power and electricity, heating, ventilation and sanitation, and architecture sectors.[9] In the database, only 10 proposals (of 458) were submitted in a consortium with contractors and 18 proposals were submitted directly to a contractor that already had a contract for a client. In the latter case, the contracts between the CF and contractor were mostly negotiated. One important reason for the trend of TCFs becoming more independent is that the increased pressure on prices for engineering services from local TCFs has meant that such services can be procured more cheaply in the host country. As the TCFs from developed countries have been forced to focus more on management services, the traditional bonds with contractors have become weaker (see Section 7.2).

In Section 2.2, it was argued that a specific reason for TCFs to be separated from the contractors is that the client or financier needs an independent firm that can evaluate different contractors' tender documents and supervise the contractor when the investment project is implemented. Svensson (1997), however, concluded that there are strong networks between TCFs and contractors— especially if they originate from the same country. Swedish TCFs, for example, procure 45% of the client's contractor services and investment materials from Swedish suppliers. Although the Swedish contractors and investment material suppliers—for example, ABB, Ericsson, Tetra Laval and Atlas Copco—are very strong in the international market, this percentage is surely much higher than these firms' world market shares, and also higher than would be the case if TCFs from other countries were responsible for the procurement of contractor services. A strong relationship between TCFs and contractors originating from the same countries has also been empirically observed by Sharma and Keller (1993).

Theoretically, there are two explanations for strong networks developing between TCFs and contractors. First, the quality and function of a system or plant cannot be evaluated before the construction or installation is completed. A large set of services and components will be purchased from different

---

[9] Recently, SWECO founded a consortium (Swedish Water Corporation), together with Swedish contractors and operators in the water sector, to coordinate their efforts when operating abroad. However, one will have to wait and see how this cooperation works.

suppliers for the implementation of this stage, and these services cannot be withdrawn when they have been executed. To minimize risks, a natural choice would be a contractor the TCF has previous experience with and confidence in. In the domestic market, the TCFs have often worked together with, or supervised, domestic contractors. These groups of firms mostly have similar formal education of their personnel, similar views on technical problems, and, above all, the same experience from the domestic market. Furthermore, the TCF has more knowledge about domestic equipment, components and services than about the foreign equivalents. It is therefore not surprising that the TCF suggests the investment contract to a contractor originating from the same country as the TCF when similar bids from different contractors are offered. As the TCF becomes more experienced with foreign markets, however, it will more often make contact with foreign contractors and investment material suppliers and cooperate with them. In other words, one can expect that the dependence on domestic contractors becomes less as the TCF develops more international experience.

Second, the TCF sometimes is assigned tasks by a contractor during the implementation phase in an investment project. The advantage here for the TCF is to be directly consulted by the contractor, implying that the TCF can avoid costs for information seeking and tendering. At the same time, the TCF can receive a higher sales volume in a project for which it earlier may have implemented feasibility studies and preliminary design in the precontract phase, and thereby use scope economies. From the contractor's point of view, it is convenient and time saving to consult a firm that has participated in the precontract phase when detailed design is going to be implemented. This TCF may, however, later be pressed to recommend the contractor for another project when contractor services are going to be purchased. It is even possible that informal groups of contractors, TCFs and investment material suppliers are created to work up foreign markets. This should be common in turnkey projects where the TCFs' services is only a small part of the whole project.

8.5 Government Assistance and Subsidies

One frequently used strategy by CFs operating abroad is to be assisted by government authorities or other export-promoting organizations in the home country, for example, the Ministry for Foreign Affairs and the national trade councils. Such authorities assist with lobbying, market observation, project information and miscellaneous advice. The purpose of this assistance is, of course, to create employment in the home country and to let firms from the home country acquire more experiences and reference assignments and upgrade their knowledge base. When the exporting firms do not pay full price for the assistance, one can consider this as a kind of subsidy that will distort competition. As a group, the government authorities from different developed countries will then not contribute to the export performance of all CFs originating in these countries, but it is rather a zero-sum game. There is, however, motivation for a specific country to give such assistance. If the authorities of other countries give assistance to "their" firms and we do not assist "our" firms, their firms will gain market shares at the expense of our firms.

In the Swedish case, the Ministry for Foreign Affairs has increased its efforts substantially during recent years and has placed persons at the largest multilateral development agencies with the purpose of observing potential export projects, and lobbying for Swedish firms.[10] The ministry has also many embassies abroad that are coordinated in export promotion activities and in a specific division—Office for Project Exports—that focuses on exports of goods and services to investment projects abroad.

The Swedish Trade Council is a semigovernment/private organization, whose task is to promote Swedish exports. For consulting exports, the council gives information and news on the Internet about international projects and tenders procured and financed by Sida or multilateral development agencies. According to interviews with key persons at the firms in the sample, the role as information publisher of potential international projects is still important, but the CFs can nowadays find this information directly via the Internet on the web sites of the multilateral development agencies. Lobbying and sending delegations to multilateral development agencies, clients and other decision makers in the host country have instead become a more important type of assistance for the exporting CFs, especially for the large CFs. The Swedish Trade Council also arranges seminars to which key persons from multilateral development agencies are invited, and the council assists with information about tender rules for different multilateral development agencies. Also, the Swedish Trade Council has foreign offices that are used when assisting exporting firms.

The Swedish Trade Council administers a government fund from which the council pays direct subsidies covering the tender costs for CFs that compete for projects within the aid programs of the EU. A requirement to receive this subsidy is that the CF must be short-listed (invited). Up to 0.1 MSEK is paid for a specific tender, but not more than 35% of the total tender costs. This subsidy will, in the first place, favor small CFs that otherwise would not be able to take on the fixed costs to learn the tender rules of the EU funds. A reason for paying these subsidies is that other developed countries also pay tender cost subsidies

---

[10] The ministry has placed one person in New York (WB and IDB), one person in London (EBRD), two persons in Brussels (EU funds) and one person in Manila (AsDB).

to their CFs (e.g., Denmark and Norway, but not necessarily to EU-financed projects). Another purpose for subsidizing tender costs of EU-financed projects, is that the Swedish export-promoting organizations may desire to give priority to the internationalization of small and medium-sized Swedish CFs. This is perhaps not an optimal strategy, however, because small CFs will not be able to operate abroad in the long run anyway, as was suggested in Chapters 3 and 4. First, they cannot use scope economies as much as large CFs can. Second, they will have fixed costs for learning the tender rules of all other multilateral development agencies (in addition to the EU funds). Long-term foreign operations of these small CFs will therefore require continuous subsidies from the Swedish government.

8.6 Swedish Consulting Firms and Multilateral Development Agencies

Swedish CFs have in general had a weak performance in the consulting market financed by multilateral development agencies during the last decades. For the Nordic Development Fund (NDF), a multilateral development agency where only CFs originating in the Nordic countries are allowed to participate in the tenders, Danish, Norwegian and Finnish CFs have obtained 35% to 40%, 25% to 35% and 20% to 25%, respectively, of the contract values during recent years. Swedish CFs have only been awarded 10% to 15% of the contract values during the same period (NDF, 1999). This is not a good performance, especially if one considers that Sweden is considerably larger than each of the other three Nordic countries for number of inhabitants, GDP and size of the domestic consulting sector. An appropriate proportion for the Swedish CFs in the NDF assistance program would be around 35%. The problem is not only that the volume of awarded contracts is low, it seems also as if Swedish CFs do not participate in the tenders to the extent they should. For example, Table A.8 (Appendix A) shows that only 6 of 358 Swedish tender documents in competition were submitted to Nordic development agencies.

The performance by the Swedish CFs is no better in EU-financed projects, as can be seen in Table 8.3. Swedish CFs were only awarded 1.4% and 1.2%, respectively, of the contract values financed by EU-PHARE and -TACIS in the late 1990s. These figures should be compared to Sweden's share of GDP in the EU-15 area, which is 2.4%. One of the reasons for the weak performance in the EU-financed market is that Sweden has only been a member of the EU since 1995. It takes time to learn the bureaucratic tender procedures of the EU funds. However, Austria and Finland, which also became members in 1995, have been more successful than Sweden and have each obtained around 3.5% of PHARE's

Table 8.3. Consulting contracts in Eastern Europe financed by EU divided on supplying countries between 1995 and 1998 in MEUR and percent.

Supplying country	PHARE 1996-97		TACIS 1995-98	
	MEUR	%	MEUR	%
Sweden	8.6	1.2	20.9	1.2
Finland	23.6	3.3	46.9	2.8
Austria	27.2	3.8	25.0	1.5
United Kingdom	157.3	22.0	n.a.	n.a.
Belgium	92.9	13.0	n.a.	n.a.
France	57.2	8.0	n.a.	n.a.
Germany	64.4	9.0	n.a.	n.a.
Denmark	65.1	9.1	n.a.	n.a.
Total budget	715	---	1,697	---

Note: n.a. = not available. *Source*: Swedish Delegation at European Union (1999).

contract values, and 1.5% and 2.8%, respectively, of TACIS' contract values during the same period.[11] Notably, Belgian CFs have a large share of the PHARE contracts. Because tendering for an EU project requires presentation of the proposal in Brussels, the tenderers will receive travel and other costs that they have to pay themselves. CFs from Belgium and nearby countries will therefore have a cost advantage compared with CFs that originate from more peripheral EU countries.

In Table 8.4, consulting contracts financed by the World Bank (including only IBRD and IDA) and AsDB are distributed by supplying countries.[12] The shares by Swedish CFs on less than 1% of the contract values do not, of course, represent a good performance—although it is a better performance than that for EU funds because CFs from more countries are allowed to participate when the World Bank and AsDB finance the projects. Comparable countries like the Netherlands, Denmark, the United Kingdom and Switzerland have a considerably better performance when taking the size of the supplying countries into account.[13]

---

[11] The statistics on awarded contracts for implementing CFs across countries is, however, not fully reliable, because only the head CF, which is responsible for the EU fund, is included in the statistics. In general, the EU funds require cooperation between implementing organizations from at least three different member countries in the EU.

[12] Each year the total amount of consulting contracts is around 880 MUSD. According to unofficial sources, however, the World Bank procured consulting services for as much as 3.8 billion USD in 1998, including IFC, different bilateral consulting funds administered by the bank and funds for technical assistance.

[13] British CFs have advantages for language, dominating international British technical standards and business relations with ex-colonies.

Table 8.4. Consulting contracts financed by the World Bank and AsDB divided on supplying countries between 1967 and 1998 (disbursements) in MUSD (current prices) and percent.

Supplying country	World Bank (%)	Asian Development Bank					
		Ordinary capital resources and Asian development fund combined (%)				Technical assistance (%)	
	1997-98	1967-76	1977-86	1987-96	1997-98	1995-96	1997-98
Sweden	0.9	0.1	0.1	1.0	0.9	1.2	0.8
Denmark	1.4	1.6	2.0	1.8	1.4	2.4	1.7
Norway	0.9	0.0	0.4	0.1	1.9	0.3	0.8
Finland	0.5	0.0	0.6	0.3	2.2	0.3	1.2
United Kingdom	16.1	3.4	14.3	11.4	7.1	19.3	11.2
France	9.5	4.2	2.9	4.2	8.8	3.2	0.8
Germany	3.6	14.0	3.5	5.9	5.2	1.8	2.2
Italy	4.4	9.4	3.0	2.5	2.1	0.1	0.6
Netherlands	3.3	3.2	2.5	1.0	4.3	3.0	4.8
Belgium	0.9	0.4	0.1	0.0	0.0	0.2	0.2
Austria	0.2	0.6	0.2	0.2	0.0	0.0	0.0
Switzerland	1.8	0.8	6.0	4.7	3.0	0.8	0.9
Spain	0.8	0.0	0.0	0.0	0.0	0.3	0.0
Portugal	1.1	n.m.	n.m.	n.m.	n.m.	n.m.	n.m.
Ireland	1.6	n.m.	n.m.	n.m.	n.m.	n.m.	n.m.
United States	20.7	31.1	19.6	10.5	15.0	22.1	23.5
Canada	6.5	7.0	7.0	3.9	7.4	9.9	10.5
Australia	2.6	4.6	2.9	4.7	7.6	12.2	14.8
Japan	1.4	11.4	13.4	5.8	3.9	1.6	1.8
Other developed	1.4	3.2	5.0	2.6	1.2	4.6	5.2
Emerging markets	20.4	5.0	16.5	39.4	28.0	16.7	19.0
Total (%)	100.0	100.0	100.0	100.0	100.0	100.0	100.0
Total (MUSD)	1,760.0	93.3	482.8	1,393.5	348.3	250.8	275.4

Note: The World Bank includes only IBRD and IDA. Total purchases of consulting services by the whole World Bank group in 1997-98 should be around 7.6 billion USD. n.m. = not member of the bank. *Source*: World Bank, (1997, 1998a) and AsDB (1997, 1998a).

In Table 8.5, the success ratios for proposals submitted to AsDB by Nordic CFs are shown. All of the success ratios are below average. A normal success ratio would be between 14% and 20%, because five to seven CFs are usually short-listed and allowed to tender. Noticeably, only the Danish CFs participate in AsDB-financed tenders to a large extent (195 proposals have been submitted during a five-year period).

Table 8.5. Success ratios for Nordic CFs when tendering for projects financed by AsDB between 1992 and 1996 in number and percent.

Supplying country	AsDB 1992-96		
	Number of awarded contracts	Number of proposals	Success ratio (%)
Sweden	12	87	14
Denmark	19	195	10
Norway	3	47	6
Finland	7	57	12

Source: AsDB (1998b).

Although some Swedish CFs are successful abroad, as discussed in Section 8.2, one has to explain why Swedish CFs are weak as a group in the market financed by multilateral development agencies. Private Swedish CFs are especially weak. This does not mean that Swedish CFs have less capacity or that the Swedish professionals have less competence or experience than their foreign competitors, but rather that the Swedish CFs may use the wrong market strategies and may not use all available possibilities, or, alternatively, may not have the same conditions for succeeding as do their foreign competitors. As can be seen in Section A.3 (Appendix A), Swedish CFs are considerably less internationalized than their Nordic competitors.

A key person employed in a multilateral development agency—who wished to be anonymous—suggests several reasons for the Swedish CFs to be less successful than CFs from similar European countries when tendering for projects financed by multilateral development agencies. First, Swedish CFs give less precise specifications in their tender documents for how tasks will be solved in the projects. Second, Swedish CFs have less experienced and less educated team leaders, who are not skilled at composing good teams. Third, the state-owned Swedish CFs are less skilled in marketing—especially marketing that is directed at the clients.[14]

There are two structural problems in the Swedish consulting sector, which likely can explain the weak performance by the Swedish CFs in the international market financed by multilateral development agencies. The first is associated with many investment subsidies in Sweden. Since the 1960s, CFs in other European countries have had a more limited demand, and fewer government subsidies, in their domestic infrastructure market than that faced by the Swedish

---

[14] He also mentions a fourth reason: Sida focuses less on purchasing of consulting services compared with bilateral development agencies from similar countries, implying that Swedish CFs will have fewer reference assignments when tendering for projects financed by multilateral development agencies. However, this was not true when comparing Sida and Danida in Table 4.3.

CFs. The foreign CFs have, therefore, been forced to seek business opportunities abroad at an early stage to survive, at the same time that the Swedish CFs have operated in a sheltered domestic market. Therefore, the foreign CFs obtained a strong advantage in reference assignments, long-term relationships with foreign clients, establishment of permanent offices abroad and ability to seek financing from different development agencies, compared with the Swedish CFs. The professionals employed by the foreign CFs thereby have curricula vitae with more merit. The losses caused by these subsidies cannot be regained by the Swedish CFs.

The second structural problem in the Swedish consulting sector, as analyzed in Chapter 7, is associated with the existence of state-owned CFs. The state-owned CFs block the private CF from hiring professionals with management skills employed by state-owned operators. This explains why private Swedish CFs have more problems in hiring experienced team leaders than do their foreign competitors, and why the Swedish consulting sector has not gone through a necessary reconfiguration where both engineering and management services can be supplied by the same CFs. A closer look at the performance by private and state-owned Swedish CFs uncovers the information that around 35% to 40% of the Swedish contracts financed by multilateral development agencies are awarded to state-owned CFs. This share is probably less than 10% for state-owned CFs from other developed countries. The unfair competition from state-owned CFs in Sweden has gone the furthest in the market for land-surveying services, where Swedesurvey used the subsidies from the parent, and blocked the possibility for private CFs to hire professionals, to such an extent that the private CFs supplying similar services were forced out of business. The same pattern can be observed in the market for telecom and aviation services, where the presence of Swedtel and Swedavia have inhibited private CFs from operating abroad.[15] Thus, a situation has arisen in Sweden implying that different skills are controlled by different CFs. Marketing skills and knowledge about the procurement rules of multilateral development agencies can be found in the private CFs, whereas the management professionals demanded by these agencies are only available for state-owned CFs. This Swedish character explains the weak performance by Swedish CFs in the market financed by multilateral development agencies, in particular, the EU funds.

As was discussed in Section 6.3, Sida and the multilateral development agencies demand different skills of the individual professionals that are going to implement the tasks in the projects—long experience and high education,

---

[15] Furthermore, unlike private Swedish CFs, private foreign CFs have not needed to compete with in-house professionals of state-owned operators in the domestic market and have thereby obtained more domestic reference assignments before they entered the foreign market.

respectively. This may imply that the Swedish professionals that implement projects financed by Sida have the "wrong" characteristics when multilateral development agencies procure consulting services, thereby partly explaining the weak Swedish performance in the market financed by these agencies. Finally, there are other explanations of a more speculative nature for the weak performance by Swedish CFs. For example, the Swedish professionals are seldom as specialized as professionals in other developed countries, meaning that they often get low points in the evaluations of international projects. Taxes are higher in Sweden than in most other developed countries—especially taxes on labor. Since the labor costs account for around 70% to 80% of the CF's total costs (excluding reimbursements), high taxes can have large implications for international competitiveness. Not surprisingly, Swedish CFs have seldom the best financial offer when tendering for projects in international competition.

8.7 Summary

This chapter analyzed various successful strategies chosen by CFs and mistakes made by them in the international market. A strategy applied by many CFs is to focus on specific host countries. One advantage is that the list of reference assignments can be refreshed at a lower cost than if the CF tries to win contracts in several new countries, because the probability is higher that the firm will be invited for more tenders if it has previous experience with the host country. When contracts become more frequent in a country, a representative office can be established as a support to the export strategy for two purposes: to develop networks with local CFs and decision makers, and to develop and maintain contacts with previous and potential clients. Such an office will not yield any direct incomes, but can be seen as a host country-specific fixed cost that must be covered by a large sales volume. Preferably, there should be several potential clients in the host country. A representative office will increase the probability that the CF is short-listed in tenders and that the firm will win tenders when proposals have been submitted. The empirical analysis supports the hypothesis that the CFs submit more proposals in countries where a representative office is established than in countries with a permanent office or no office at all.

For employment strategies, the CFs can choose between having permanent employees or hiring professionals on a project basis. A hiring strategy has many advantages. First, the CF can more easily match the demand for services with resources (professionals) available, and it does not need to pay salaries to professionals who have no tasks; that is, overcapacity is avoided. Second, the CF will obtain flexibility in the sense that it can adapt itself to new demand trends in the market simply by hiring new kinds of professionals. These two advantages were used maximally by one of the CFs in the sample—Hifab International—when the international demand trend shifted toward management services in recent years. There are also disadvantages with a hiring strategy: the professionals must be hired in competition with other CFs, and the professionals must take a leave from their permanent job, meaning that the CF may be in a position of having a contract but no professionals. Furthermore, a CF that applies a hiring strategy will have problems accumulating and diffusing knowledge in the firm, because the hired professionals seldom meet each other and will return to their permanent employers when the projects are completed.

Mistakes are common in the international market. First, consortiums are founded by CFs that do not supply complementary services. Second, international consulting is done in a noncontinuous way, meaning that old reference assignments will be worthless because the value of such assignments will deteriorate over time. Third, tendering only for large profitable projects is not recommended, because the competition for such projects is fierce. Unless the CF has previous experience with the client, the CF will probably lose the tender. It is important also to tender for small projects, even though these projects are not profitable. This should be seen as a way of marketing aimed at new clients. Fourth, many CFs put too little effort into projects financed by multilateral development agencies. Since these agencies have tender rules that are associated with fixed learning costs for the CFs, many contracts must be awarded for each agency.

The performance by Swedish CFs in the market financed by multilateral development agencies has been weak. There are two main explanations for this situation. First, the domestic market has during several decades faced more investment subsidies than have other European countries. The Swedish CFs have therefore lagged behind competitors in other countries for international reference assignments, experience with the tender rules of multilateral development agencies, and long-term relationships with local clients. Second, the Swedish market for management professionals is blocked by state-owned CFs, implying that private Swedish CFs are not able to hire professionals with skills that are demanded by the multilateral development agencies. In principle, marketing skills and knowledge about procurement rules of the multilateral development agencies are controlled by the private Swedish CFs, whereas the state-owned CFs control the management professionals demanded by these agencies. The result is that neither private nor state-owned Swedish CFs win contracts financed by these agencies to any large extent.

Chapter 9

CONCLUSIONS

In this book, I theoretically and empirically analyzed several issues related to cross-border operations of consulting firms (CFs). These issues include: 1) competitive factors and strategies that influence the outcome of international tender evaluations in competition; 2) the choice of entry mode when penetrating a foreign market; 3) the role and consequences of development agencies operating in the international consulting market; 4) to which extent, and under which conditions, knowledge is transferred to emerging markets when consulting projects are implemented; 5) the extent and consequences of the emergence of new services, like management services, in the international market; and 6) the consequences of state-owned CFs operating in the market for private CFs. Several other issues were also investigated, such as the advantages and disadvantages of hiring professionals on a project basis compared with having permanent employees, and the performance by Swedish CFs in the market financed by multilateral development agencies.

The analysis was based on two premises. First, I developed theories about the CFs and their behavior from empirical observations of the characteristics of consulting services, CFs and clients. Second, a unique database on individual proposals submitted abroad by Swedish CFs was collected and used in the empirical analyses, where I tested the theories and the aforementioned issues. Although the data covers Swedish CFs—both management and technical CFs—operating in the infrastructure sectors, I argue that most of the analyses and conclusions in the book are valid also for CFs originating in other countries and operating in other sectors, because most CFs and consulting services share the same characteristics. Here, I present some of the main conclusions, whereas more detailed conclusions can be found in the summary of each chapter.

One central issue analyzed in the book concerns the factors that determine the selection of a CF—both in the first competitive step, where CFs are invited to participate in the tender, and in the final selection of one CF when tender documents are evaluated (Chapter 6). The theoretical starting point was that consulting services cannot be evaluated before they have been purchased—a typical problem with asymmetric information where the seller knows more than the buyer. "Signals" to the client about the firm's competence and experience and that of its employees should then be important. Furthermore, if the client has previous experience with the CF, he or she will know something about the quality of the services and the capabilities of the CF. Thus, repeat purchases from the same supplier and strong long-term relationships between CFs and their clients should be frequent. These relationships take time to develop and are difficult to break for outsider CFs. The long-term relationships are reinforced by the fact that most consulting services require direct contact between the CF and the client, and by the fact that they are jointly produced by these agents. Communication and cooperation are important factors that are also difficult to evaluate a priori.

The empirical analysis supports the view that signals in the form of general experiences of the whole firm, such as the experience with the host country and with similar projects abroad, and long-term relationships in the form of previous contracts for the client seem to determine which CFs are invited to tender. Although these factors are significant across all financing groups, the more the client is allowed to influence the invitation, the more important these factors become. When detailed proposals are submitted in the second step, long-term relationships between the supplier and the client—for example, previous contracts with the client (repeat purchases) or whether the CF visited the client or not—are the most important determinants. Previous contracts may increase the probability of winning the contract by as much as 20 to 25 percentile units. It was concluded that the CF visits the client to affect the decision making rather than as a source of information about the project so that a better proposal can be submitted. The experience and education level of the team leader, representing employee-specific signals, also have a significant impact on the firm's probability of winning the contract. However, signals representing the experience of the whole firm do not have any significant impact on the outcome in the second step.

The most interesting difference across financing groups is that long-term relationships are important for commercial, Sida and EU projects but not for projects financed by other multilateral development agencies. The latter agencies seem to have stricter rules for procurement of consulting services. Notably, the long-term relationship factors are given zero points in the tender evaluations of all development agencies. It is, however, not surprising that long-term relationships are important in the latter tender evaluations and that these evaluations have become more similar to those in the commercial market, because the clients have more to say about the selection of supplier in projects financed by development agencies in recent years. The fact that the long-term relationships have such a strong influence on the outcome is an indication that in some (but far from all) of the projects the client has predecided which supplier to choose. The client invites several CFs to tender for two reasons. First, the client may be forced to do so by the financier. Second, the client wants to subject a previously hired CF to competitive pressure. Since many of the development agencies do not seem to follow their strict tender rules, a policy implication is that these agencies can either skip, or at least relax, their strict rules, or increase the sanctions associated with violations of the rules. For negotiated contracts, previous experience with the client and thereby repeat purchases are even more prominent than for projects procured in competition.

Another principal question concerns the choice of entry mode in foreign markets (Chapter 3). The theoretical starting points were: 1) consulting exports are associated with high reimbursements compared with local sales because the professionals must travel to the host country; 2) one of the largest problems to solve for the CFs is to match professionals available with demand for the firm's services, because these firms offer the client flexibility by hiring out professionals on a project basis; and 3) the strength of local long-term relationships and local competitors is decisive. High reimbursements inhibit CFs from exporting to developed markets where local competition is strong. Establishment of greenfield offices in such markets is not recommended because of the strong local long-term relationships. Thus, acquisition is the only profitable alternative when entering a developed market. In emerging markets there are few clients, meaning that demand is unstable. CFs from developed countries are therefore forced to move from one project to another in different emerging markets when following the sector-specific demand shocks. Establishment of permanent offices in such markets is therefore a risky strategy. At the same time, local competitiveness and long-term relationships are weak, meaning that exports seem to be an appropriate strategy. Since the competitors from other developed countries also have high reimbursement costs, these costs are not as important in this situation. However, when local demand is stable and local competition is weak, as in the telecom sector, the establishment of a greenfield office is an appropriate strategy.

The empirical analysis strongly supports the view that developed markets are entered by acquiring local CFs, whereas emerging markets are supplied through exports. In fact, as much as 90% of the consulting exports are directed to the latter markets. Exporting to developed markets is possible as an exception if the orders come from a previous international client that operates in the local market. Furthermore, there is a significant difference between the permanent offices that are established in developed markets and the few that are set up in emerging markets. The former operate independent of exports, whereas most of the latter are used in combination with exports from the home country. Because the pressure on prices for engineering services has increased during recent years in emerging markets, such services are subcontracted either to independent local firms or to the CF's own local offices, and the more complex tasks are implemented by professionals from the home country. A permanent office in an emerging market should be minority owned to reduce the risks caused by the sector-specific demand shocks. If the local employees own a majority share, they will have more incentives to put extra effort into winning contracts on their own. Local presence in the form of a permanent office has a strong positive influence on the outcome in the tender evaluations.

In emerging markets, representative offices are often set up to support the export strategy, for example to develop networks with local CFs and decision makers, and to develop and maintain contacts with previous and potential clients. Such an office can be seen as a host country-specific fixed cost and requires that the CF has a large sales volume in that host country over which to spread the fixed costs. Preferably, there should then be several potential clients in the host country. A representative office will in turn increase the probability that the CF is short-listed in tenders and that the firm will win tenders when proposals have been submitted. A strategy applied by many CFs is to focus on specific host countries, which makes it possible for the CF to have representative offices. Another advantage with this focusing strategy is that the list of reference assignments can be refreshed at a lower cost than if the CF tries to win contracts in several new countries, because the probability is higher that the firm will be invited for more tenders if it has previous experience with the host country. The empirical analysis supports the hypothesis that the CFs focus on specific countries and submit more proposals in countries where a representative office is established than in countries with a permanent office or no office at all (Chapter 8).

Furthermore, it was observed that the CFs are the prototype of knowledge-based firms, because they collect information about technology, management, laws, and so on, that are packaged and sold as services (Chapter 5). The CFs' only factor of production is the knowledge or human capital embodied in the employees. Knowledge transfer to the clients and other firms involved in the projects should be particularly high and intensive when consulting services are implemented, because: 1) CFs are highly knowledge intensive; 2) production of the services often requires close cooperation between the CF and the client; and 3) services can seldom be patented, meaning that the client and other firms can freely replicate the services in their own projects. Development agencies have paid increasing attention to this fact, and focus nowadays more on purchasing of consulting services instead of financing large turnkey projects in emerging markets. The idea is that the clients and local firms in the host countries will learn to replicate the services executed by the CFs from developed countries. As much as 60% to 90% of the consulting exports from developed to emerging markets are financed by such agencies.

To make the knowledge transfer effective, training of, and cooperation with, the client or local firms are necessary elements in the project. Since the transfer will decrease the knowledge gap between international and local CFs and thereby make the knowledge base of the international CFs less valuable, these

CFs have no incentives to train, or transfer know-how to, local firms. This must instead be induced by the client or the development agencies. The international CFs must then continuously upgrade their knowledge bases if they wish to stay competitive in the international market. The transferees, on the other hand, must be able to assimilate the knowledge. This capacity can be improved through costly training. In fact, empirical analysis shows that the development agencies, rather than the client, include training in the projects. Furthermore, the lower the development level of the host country, the more likely training is included in the project, whereas the higher the development level of the host country, the more frequently cooperation with local CFs occurs. In fact, in the least developed countries, there are seldom any local CFs with which to cooperate. Because those in the poorest countries have a low ability to learn, it is expected that the knowledge gap between the least and most developed emerging markets will increase as consulting projects are implemented. The latter countries may even catch up with the developed countries.

Apart from the transfer of knowledge, financing of consulting projects by the development agencies increases the welfare of the host country, of course, because the services in themselves have value for the client (Chapter 4). Furthermore, because the knowledge gap is large between CFs from developed countries and clients in emerging markets, these agencies have to assist in preproject identifications, negotiations and postproject evaluations; otherwise the CFs may try to cheat the clients in some way. The development agencies also have several roles for the international CFs. For example, the risk that clients with low financial credibility will not pay for implemented projects is reduced for the CF, implying that competition will be stronger than in commercial projects, and that CFs will sell more services to emerging markets than otherwise would happen; in fact, many of the projects would not be initiated at all without this financing. The agencies also function as market observers of potential projects for the international CFs.

When bilateral development agencies like Sida finance consulting projects, there are fewer tenderers because the development assistance is tied. These agencies therefore function as spearheads for CFs from the same country into new markets, but they are even more important in this role when the CFs win the first contract for new clients. However, Sida gives priority to the experience of the proposed staff, whereas the other development agencies and the client seem to favor the education level. A consequence is that the regrowth of professionals in Sweden is inhibited and Sida's role in spearheading the Swedish CFs into new markets is limited because multilateral development agencies require other skills of the staff than what Sida requires. Finally, the procurement rules of bi- and multilateral development agencies differ from each other in several respects. These different rules can therefore be regarded as fixed costs specific for each agency that the international CFs have to learn about, meaning that, in some sense, scale is necessary to operate abroad.

Another observation is that management services are more frequently included in international projects, especially when development agencies are involved (Chapter 7). Engineering services are to a higher degree procured from local TCFs. This trend is caused by local TCFs having learned to replicate engineering services as a consequence of more training from, and cooperation with, international CFs. Moreover, the worldwide trend toward privatization and market deregulation in the infrastructure sectors also explains the shift to management services. There are several consequences for the international CFs. First, they have to acquire new skills and recruit professionals who can supply the new services. Second, cooperation with inexpensive local TCFs that can supply bulk design services will increase in importance. Third, a larger part of the time will be spent in the host country when supplying management services because they take the form of labor services. Thus, costs for reimbursements will be higher, but costs for offices at home will be lower. Fourth, the fact that contacts and cooperation with the client will be more frequent implies that social competence of the professionals, good communication with the clients, and marketing will become more important. Fifth, less engineering services implies that the interdependence between TCFs and contractors originating in developed countries will become weaker in the international market.

In Sweden, private CFs have problems recruiting management professionals, which is closely related to the presence of state-owned CFs. The latter CFs have exclusive dealing contracts with their parent operators, and can thereby hire management professionals on a project basis from their parent companies. Because the private CFs are not allowed to hire professionals from these operators, it can be argued that the state-owned CFs enjoy an unfair competitive advantage compared with the private CFs. Since the state-owned CFs do not pay extra for the privilege, they are cross-subsidized by their parent operators. This kind of privileged position is called "predation by putting rivals at a cost disadvantage," and will cause the private CFs to have higher search costs when hiring professionals and larger restrictions on their service production. It is not likely that the combination of an operator and a CF in one firm is an effective way to organize production, because similar combined firms rarely exist in the private sector, but is rather a sign of government inefficiency of the operator. As the state-owned CFs in principle blockade the Swedish infrastructure market for management professionals, these firms prevent a necessary restructuring of the consulting sector. It is also likely that the existence of these CFs decreases rather than increases the competition in the consulting market, particularly when Sida procures consulting services. The problems could easily be solved by allowing *any* CF to hire professionals from the operators. The operators would then probably earn a higher profit.

In Chapter 8, it was noted that Swedish CFs, for a long time, have had a weak performance in the market financed by multilateral development agencies, especially by EU funds. These agencies include a lot of management components in their projects. The problem in Sweden is that the exclusive dealing contracts between the state-owned CFs and their parent operators have caused the competence of marketing and knowledge about the tender rules of development agencies, on the one hand, and the control over management professionals, on the other hand, to be separated in different CFs. This is likely the main reason for the weak performance by Swedish CFs in the market financed by multilateral development agencies, especially by the EU funds. The performance could be improved by simply letting any CF hire management professionals from the state-owned operators.

Considering employment strategies, the CFs can either choose between a strategy with permanent employees or hiring professionals on a project basis (Chapter 8). With a hiring strategy, the CF can more easily match the demand for services with the professionals available, and it does not need to pay salaries to professionals who have no tasks; that is, overcapacity is avoided. Furthermore, the CF obtains flexibility in the sense that it can adapt itself to new demand trends in the market, simply by hiring new kinds of professionals. These two advantages have been used to a maximum by one of the CFs in the sample —Hifab International—when the international demand trend shifted toward management services in recent years. There are also disadvantages with a hiring strategy. The professionals must be hired in competition with other CFs, and the professionals must take leave, meaning that the CF may face a position in which it has a contract but no professionals. A CF that applies a hiring strategy will have problems accumulating and diffusing knowledge in the firm, because the hired professionals seldom meet each other and will return to their permanent employers when the projects are completed.

Finally, there is a need for further research in the area of CFs and their foreign operations. For example, whether the strong long-term relationships between the CFs and their clients are bound to the CFs or to the professionals employed by the CFs should be investigated. Another interesting process would be to develop a method that measures the actual strength and effectiveness of knowledge transfer to emerging markets. It would also be interesting to analyze some of the issues addressed in this book from the client's or financier's point of view, such as the procurement of consulting services in competition, where one could compare proposals submitted from different CFs to the same tender. However, even more sophisticated databases are needed in such cases.

Appendix A

SWEDISH AND NORDIC CONSULTING EXPORTS

In this appendix, we provide basic empirical observations of Swedish consulting firms (CFs) and their foreign operations during the 1990s. Comparisons are also made with CFs from other Nordic countries. We start by describing the databases for firm-level and individual proposals, the sample criteria and the collection. Thereafter, the history of foreign operations for Swedish CFs during the last two decades is presented. In the rest of the appendix, we provide descriptive statistics for Swedish CFs and their tender documents.

A.1 Databases and Sample Selection

With the purpose of creating two databases that will be used in the empirical analysis of this book, two different questionnaires—described in detail in Appendix B—were sent out to, and filled in by, Swedish CFs operating in the infrastructure sectors. The first survey is at the firm level and includes statistics on the foreign operations of CFs distributed by region, sector and financing for the years 1992, 1994 and 1996. The other, and more important, survey is based on individual tender documents or proposals submitted abroad between 1995 and 1997. In it I have collected both awarded and lost tenders. This database contains information about each CF's experience with the host country, the client and similar assignments abroad. It also includes statistics on the strategies undertaken by the tenderer, for example, whether the CF visited the client in connection with the tender, the education level and international experience of the CF's suggested team leader for the project and whether the CF planned to cooperate with other international or local CFs. Furthermore, information is available about the financing, the sector, the type of client and the kind of services included in the project. The location of the CF's foreign offices were collected separately. Finally, face-to-face interviews were undertaken with key persons working in the sector.

The sample criteria for a firm to be included in the databases are that the CF must: 1) have consulting as a dominating activity; 2) sell services in the infrastructure sectors; and 3) have submitted at least one tender document abroad during the 1995 to 1997 period. The questionnaires were sent out to thirty-eight CFs. Thirty-one CFs fulfilled the sample criteria *and* participated in the investigation. Three CFs did not fulfill the sample criteria and four CFs did not wish to participate, either because of limited time to spend on filling in questionnaires or refusal to give information about tender documents.[1] The 31 participating firms account, however, for more than 90% of the Swedish consulting export in the infrastructure sectors and these firms and their main infrastructure sectors of operation abroad are described in Table A.1. Some of the CFs, for example, SWECO, ÅF and Hifab, have several specialized divisions or affiliates which are treated as separate CFs in the survey. This treatment will, however, not affect the analysis later in the book. When firm-level analysis is appropriate, these divisions will sometimes be aggregated as one firm in the analysis. Most of the firms in the survey are technical consulting firms (TCFs) that supply all kinds of traditional engineering services and some management services, but seven of the firms are management consulting firms (MCFs), denoted with an asterisk in the table, which only supply management services. Although not shown in the table, some of these MCFs, for example, Hifab and ISO Swedish Management Group, operate also in other sectors like the health, government administration, educational system and financial sectors. Some of the other CFs in the survey could be regarded as combinations of TCFs and MCFs. This is especially relevant for Swedtel, SweRoad and JP Consulting.

The database on individual tender documents is constructed from the firm's point of view. This means that I have statistics on competitive factors and strategies of a specific tenderer, but no information about the actions undertaken by the competitors. Only occasionally do I have information about two or more firms that have submitted proposals to the same project. A database on specific tenders with information on all tenderers would be almost impossible to collect. That would, for example, require information about foreign firms' tender documents.

A problem that arose when collecting this database was that CFs seldom have extra time to fill in hundreds of questionnaires. Therefore, I have tried to collect as many tender documents as possible from each firm, but, at the same time, I have had in mind that the sample must be representative. For the larger CFs, a list of all projects to which the firm has submitted tender documents during the period was received. After that, a random sample of proposals was selected from this list—mostly between 15% and 30% of all proposals. For the smaller CFs, a larger share of all submitted proposals was collected. It is not likely that smaller firms are heavily overrepresented for the number of tender documents, because CFs that are not included in the sample or that refused to participate are always smaller CFs, whereas all larger Swedish CFs operating in the infrastructure sectors are included. For example, the five largest exporters

---

[1] Furthermore, there should be many small CFs operating in the infrastructure sectors, but they are difficult to identify.

in the sample—Swedtel, SwedPower, SWECO, ÅF and Hifab—account for 73% (963 of 1,317 MSEK in Table A.2 below) of all exports in the firm-level database. In the detailed database, these five firms stand for 63% of all tender values (1,824 of 2,879 MSEK) and 65% of the contract values of all awarded tenders (519 of 794 MSEK).

In total, I have a sample of 458 tender documents, of which 358 are with and 100 are without competition. Most tender documents have been submitted to developing countries (274) and Eastern Europe (145), and developed markets account for less than 10% (39). For financing, Swedish International Development and Cooperation Agency (Sida) (155), multilateral development agencies (164) and commercial tenders (139) account for around 1/3 each. The selected 458 observations account for around 25% of all tender documents that the 31 firms submitted abroad during the 1995 to 1997 period. The share of awarded tenders in the sample is, not surprisingly, somewhat overestimated, because it is always easier for the firms to give information about awarded tenders than it is about lost tenders. This overestimation seems, however, to be independent of other variables such as regions, sectors or financing groups. When analyzing the relationship between the outcome of the tender evaluation and other variables, I therefore do not expect to get biased results.

When collecting firm-level sales data, a problem arose because some CFs use "the net method" (only fees) and others "the gross method" (fees plus reimbursements) in their accounts. I choose to apply the gross method, because most firms in the sample use it.[2] Revenues from real estate and capital gains and affiliated "industrial TCFs" have been excluded.[3] In both databases, all sales and tender values include therefore both fees and reimbursements.

A.2 History of Swedish Consulting Firms

In the 1960s, the Swedish economy faced a boom with adherent investments in infrastructure and industry. This meant that the domestic demand for engineering expertise and knowledge supplied by TCFs was high, and as a result the technical consulting sector experienced a period of consolidated growth. Most TCFs, therefore, concentrated their efforts in the domestic market and to some extent in the neighboring Nordic countries. Only a handful Swedish TCFs were engaged in foreign operations. In the 1970s and 1980s, many Swedish TCFs

---

[2] Accordingly, the firm-level sales by KM, SCC, Hifab and Samark have been upgraded to gross sales. In principle, this means that sales in Sweden or in permanent foreign affiliates have been upgraded by around 10% and in the case of exports by around 35% to 40%. From 1997 onward, all Swedish CFs have been required to use the gross method in their annual accounts.

[3] This means that the turnover for SWECO, J&W and ÅF has been reduced.

Table A.1. Swedish CFs included in the surveys and their main foreign infrastructure sectors of operation.

Name of the firm		Main infrastructure sectors abroad
ÅF [Ångpanneföreningen]	ÅF-Elteknik	Power and electricity
	ÅF-Energikonsult Syd	District heating, power and waste
	ÅF-Energikonsult Stockholm	District heating, power and waste
	ÅF-IPK	Forest industry (manufacturing) and environment
	ÅF-VVS Projekt	Heating, ventilation and sanitation
Bengt Dahlgren		Heating, ventilation and sanitation
FVB [Fjärrvärmebyrån]		District heating
Hifab *	Hifab International *	MS (environment, water, roads, natural resources, etc.)
	SGAB [Swedish Geological] *	Geology (natural resources)
ISO Swedish Management Group *		MS (telecom, roads, railways, manufacturing, etc.)
J&W [Jacobson & Widmark]		MS (buildings, water, energy, etc.)
JP Consulting		Forestry (natural resources) and environment
KM [Kjessler & Mannerstråhle]		Roads, environment and water
NCG [Nordic Consulting Group] *		MS (transport infrastructure, energy, water, etc.)
Samark		Hospitals (buildings)
SCC [Scandiaconsult]		MS (water, ports, airports, etc.)
SPM Consultants *		MS (energy, water, environment, etc.)

SWECO	Power and electricity
Beco	Buildings
Bloco	District heating; heating, ventilation and sanitation
Theorells	Hydro power and tunnels
SWECO Anläggning	Water, environment and roads
SWECO Viak	
Swedavia * #	Airports and aviation
SwedeRail * #	Railways
SwedPower #	Power and electricity; hydro power
Swedtel #	Telecommunication
SweRoad #	Roads
VAB Road & Rail	Roads and railways
VA-Ingenjörerna	Water
VAI VA-Projekt (former Rust VA-Projekt)	Water and waste
White Arkitekter	Buildings

Note: An asterisk (*) indicates that the firm is a management consulting firm (MCF) that does not supply any technical calculations or design services abroad. A gate (#) indicates that the firm is state owned. MS means multiple sectors. ÅF and Hifab include only those affiliates that operate in the infrastructure sectors. ÅF and ISO merged in January 1998.

were, however, forced to seek business opportunities abroad in response to the stagnation in demand for investments, especially infrastructure projects, in the domestic market. In 1982, about 60 Swedish TCFs exported services for 725 MSEK (Johanson and Sharma, 1983). At that time, many of the large Swedish TCFs had 20% to 40% of their sales in foreign markets. A conspicuous feature of this period was the concentration of exports to the oil-producing countries in the Middle East, explained by the rapidly increasing oil revenues and the undeveloped infrastructure and industry in that area. This was accompanied by a lack of local technical expertise and know-how to implement investments themselves. Another feature of the foreign operations up to the late 1980s was that almost exclusively engineering services were exported by TCFs. Export of management services and the presence of Swedish MCFs in the international market were scarce.

The overall international competition intensified as industrial stagnation continued in developed countries and forced more CFs to go abroad. Host country governments also encouraged the establishment of local TCFs in order to decrease the dependence on foreign TCFs. Hence, competition from international and local TCFs became stiff, including in the Middle East which faced decreasing oil prices from the mid-1980s. The consequences have been an increasing willingness by the international TCFs to cooperate with local TCFs, together with an increase in the importance of price competition, especially for design services. Quality, however, is still the most important factor. Partly as a result of this increased competition, Swedish TCFs have decreased their foreign operations in a stepwise manner since the mid-1980s. Many private TCFs failed when they tried to export services to commercial projects in other developing countries, with the result that the TCFs thereafter concentrated their export efforts on projects financed by development agencies. The latter projects are associated with a lower risk than are commercial projects because development agencies guarantee that the CF will be paid for implemented projects.

In the beginning of the 1980s, several Swedish technical consulting consortiums, for example, SWECO, Eastechnology, Uniconsult and Civil Defense Engineering, operated abroad and aimed at minimizing risks and marketing costs as well as pooling technical skills in international consulting. The most successful was SWECO, which in the mid-1980s was ranked as one of the five largest TCFs in the world. Other consortiums were less successful partly because of rivalry between the members (Johanson and Sharma, 1983). Since the early 1980s, however, the Swedish technical consulting sector has faced an increasing market concentration. Large TCFs have acquired other medium-sized and small TCFs, mirrored by the fact that the domestic market share of the 30 largest TCFs was 50% in 1983, and about 60% in 1995. The idea has been to diversify into new technical and geographical areas of the domestic market to counteract the industrial and investment stagnation that occurred in Sweden during the last decades. From that process, the Swedish TCFs can now provide a more complete set of services and do not complement each other to the same extent as before. The need for consortiums has, therefore, more or less vanished. Of the former consortiums only SWECO remains, but this firm is not a consortium any longer. KM left SWECO in 1996, and the other owner, VBB, changed its name to SWECO.

In the 1970s and 1980s, a number of state-owned CFs, "Swed-firms" (e.g., Swedtel, SwedPower and SweRoad), were created with the purpose of selling consulting services abroad. These firm are affiliates to state-owned operators or government ministries like Telia ("Swedish Telecom"), Vattenfall ("Swedish Hydro Power") and Swedish National Road Administration. The Swed-firms loosely cooperated in the beginning, but they do not coordinate their foreign operations any more. They have, until recently, not directly competed with the private TCFs, because to a higher degree they supply (nontechnical) management services rather than engineering services. Since most development agencies nowadays give more priority to management services in their programs, however, the private TCFs have been forced to enter this market in order to survive abroad and thereby to compete with the Swed-firms. At the same time, privately owned MCFs have turned up and taken market shares during the last 10 years. The trend from engineering toward management services is discussed in Chapter 7.

A.3 Basic Statistics on Firms

In Table A.2, domestic, foreign and export sales in 1992, 1994 and 1996 are shown for the 31 firms in the sample. They have a total turnover of 6.3 billion SEK in 1996, which is 50% to 55% of the total sales of 12 to 13 billion SEK of all Swedish CFs operating in the infrastructure sectors.[4] The proportion of exports to total sales has fluctuated at around 20% and the proportion of exports to Swedish turnover (domestic plus export sales) has been around 22% for the selected firms. Since the firms in the survey account for more than 90% of all Swedish exports in the sector, the proportion of exports to Swedish turnover for the whole sector (including Swedish CFs with no or few exports that are not

---

[4] The whole Swedish technical consulting sector had a total sales of almost 16 billion SEK in 1996 (Swedish Federation of Architects and Consulting Engineers, 1998). From this figure we exclude TCFs that solely sell engineering services to manufacturing firms (e.g., Caran, Semcon, Benima Ferator, Sigma and other firms), which had a total turnover of approximately 3 to 4 billion SEK the same year, and add MCFs operating in the infrastructure sectors, which had a total turnover of approximately 1 billion SEK.

Table A.2. Sales and exports by Swedish CFs in 1992, 1994 and 1996 and comparisons with CFs from other Nordic countries in current prices and MSEK.

Swedish CFs	1992	1994	1996
Total sales	5,031	5,166	6,321
Domestic sales	3,840	3,875	4,533
Foreign sales	1,191	1,291	1,788
of which exports from Sweden	1,042	1,118	1,292
Sales in developed countries	232	258	598
of which exports from Sweden	93	102	127
Sales in emerging markets	959	1,033	1,190
of which exports from Sweden	949	1,016	1,165

Nordic CFs		1992	1994	1996
Finnish	Domestic sales (MFIM)	1,900	1,300	1,800
	Exports from Finland (MFIM)	500	700	900
Norwegian	Domestic sales (MNOK)	c 2,100	c 2,200	2,500
	Exports from Norway (MNOK)	370	532	750
Danish	Domestic sales (MDKK)	c 2,800	c 3,200	c 3,700
(net sales)	Exports from Denmark (MDKK)	c 1,000	c 1,050	c 1,100

Note: Finland's, Norway's and Denmark's figures include all CFs that are members of SKOL (1997), R.I.F. (1997) and F.R.I. (1997), respectively. The Danish figures concern net sales. Architecture firms and sales from foreign offices are not included in the figures for the other Nordic countries.

included in the sample) should be around 12% (about 1.44 of 12.5 billion SEK).

Although domestic sales by Swedish CFs increased by 18% during the period, sales from foreign permanent offices and exports from Sweden have increased by 233% and 24%, respectively. The large expansion in sales from permanent offices abroad is explained by large acquisitions between 1994 and 1996. Acquired affiliates abroad account for almost 80% of the sales in developed countries at the same time as all sales in emerging markets, that is, developing countries and Eastern Europe, consist of exports to 98%.

A comparison with other Nordic countries shows that export by Norwegian and Finnish CFs expanded strongly during the last years, whereas export by Danish CFs is almost unchanged. In the Norwegian case, this increase is explained by the expansion in the telecom sector in developing countries and in the Finnish case by the expansion in the manufacturing sector (pulp and paper) in both developed and emerging markets. The CFs from these Nordic countries

Table A.3. Swedish sales and exports by private and state-owned CFs in 1992, 1994 and 1996 in current prices and MSEK.

	Privately owned CFs			State-owned CFs		
	1992	1994	1996	1992	1994	1996
Total sales	4,654	4,680	5,695	377	486	626
Domestic sales	3,840	3,875	4,533	0	0	0
Foreign sales	814	805	1,162	377	486	626
of which exports from Sweden	672	642	681	370	476	611
Sales in developed countries	218	239	557	14	19	41
of which exports from Sweden	79	83	86	14	19	41
Sales in emerging markets	596	566	605	363	467	585
of which exports from Sweden	593	559	595	356	457	570

Note: The state-owned firms in the sample are Swedavia, SwedeRail, SwedPower, Swedtel and SweRoad.

have relatively high export sales compared to the domestic sales. Whereas the share of exports to Swedish turnover is around 12% for the whole Swedish sector in 1996, comparable shares for Finland, Norway and Denmark are 33%, 23% and 23%, respectively.

In Table A.3, the Swedish CFs are divided into private and state-owned CFs. The Swedish export increased from 1,042 MSEK to 1,292 MSEK between 1992 and 1996. Almost all of this increase can be attributed to the four state-owned CFs that have increased their export from 370 MSEK to 611 MSEK—primarily explained by the expansion in the telecom sector as in the Norwegian case. The private CFs in the sample have also expanded during the last years in both domestic sales and sales from foreign offices, but this is explained by large acquisitions in Sweden and other developed countries. Domestic sales in the whole Swedish technical consulting sector have been relatively stable. Private export to emerging markets seems to have reached a status quo, but the figures in the table do not indicate that some firms expand strongly whereas others almost exit the foreign market. Note also that the private CFs have almost 90% of their export in emerging markets.

In Figure A.1, the Swedish CFs are sorted according to the size of their sales in emerging markets. Foreign activities vary widely across firms. Many of the large private CFs have only a fraction of their total sales, 3% to 8%, in emerging markets. Exceptions are Hifab and the smaller firms VAI VA-Projekt, JP Consulting and Samark, which all have more than 1/3 of their sales in these areas. The state-owned Swed-firms (Swedavia, SwedeRail, SwedPower, Swedtel and SweRoad) have almost as much sales in these areas as the private CFs

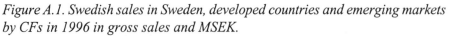

Figure A.1. Swedish sales in Sweden, developed countries and emerging markets by CFs in 1996 in gross sales and MSEK.

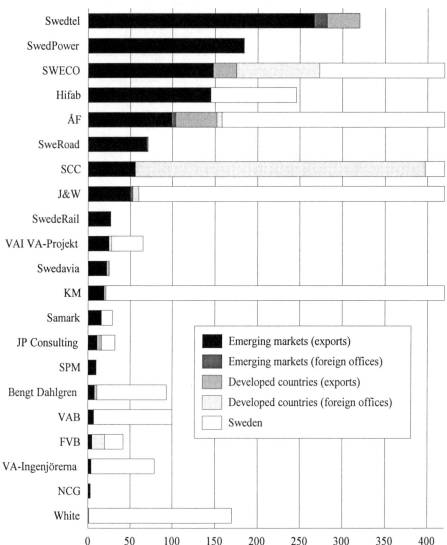

Note: SWECO includes figures for both VBB and FFNS, although these two firms did not merge until 1997. ÅF includes the affiliates listed in Table A.1 and ISO, although ÅF and ISO did not merge until 1998. The figures for SCC, KM and Hifab have been recalculated to gross sales. Revenues from capital gains and real estate are excluded from SWECO's and J&W's figures. Around 1/3 of Swedtel's export is internal export to the parent operator's foreign affiliates. SWECO had a total sales of 1,504, ÅF had 660, SCC had 1,168, J&W had 987 and KM had 597 MSEK.

together. However, around 1/3 of Swedtel's export is directed to the parent operator's majority-owned affiliates abroad, meaning that Swedtel's export in reality is 212 MSEK. In developed countries, on the other hand, SCC dominates substantially with large foreign permanent offices, and SWECO, ÅF and Swedtel account for the rest. More than 50% of the export to these markets is associated with clients originating in Sweden.

A.4 Statistics on Sectors and Regions

The Swedish CFs' foreign sales across sectors are shown in Table A.4. For total foreign sales, the telecom, transport infrastructure and energy sectors account for around 20% each and the water and environment sectors for 15% together. The difference between the sales in developed and emerging markets is, however, substantial. In the former markets, transport infrastructure dominates at 36%, and the manufacturing and building sectors have around 18% each. By contrast, the telecom and energy sectors dominate in emerging markets. The export column does not differ much from the sales column for emerging markets apart from the fact that the manufacturing sector gets 10% instead of 5% of the total.

The distribution of total exports across sectors is similar for Swedish and Norwegian firms—telecom and energy dominate. Although not shown in the table, the manufacturing sector, with the CF Jaakko Pöyry operating in the pulp and paper, accounts for as much as 60%, and the building sector for 13%, of the Finnish exports (SKOL, 1997). The exports by Swedish CFs can also be compared to that of the Swedish contractors: telecom accounts for 55%, energy for 20%, manufacturing for 17%, and transport infrastructure for 6% (Svensson, 1996). The Swedish CFs seem to be relatively strong exporters in the telecom, energy, water and environment sectors.

In Table A.5, export by the Swedish, Norwegian and Danish CFs is distributed across regions. For the former two countries, the export is almost solely directed toward emerging markets, at 90% and 97%, respectively. This structure is in line with the theory developed in Chapter 3.[5] Denmark has, on the other hand, as much as 1/3 of its export to Western Europe, which can be partly explained by architect firms that export almost 100 MDKK to Germany. (F.R.I., 1997). Also some of the export by Finnish CFs is directed toward developed markets, but the CFs are helped by the Nordic pulp and paper industry's invest-

---

[5] Most Swedish TCFs that operated abroad in 1982 had, in fact, started their foreign operations in developing countries—especially in the Middle East and Africa (Svenska Konsultföreningen, 1982).

Table A.4. Swedish and Norwegian foreign sales and exports by CFs across sectors in 1996 in percent and MSEK.

| Sector | Swedish foreign sales | | | | | | Swedish exports | | Norwegian exports |
| | Total | | Developed markets | | Emerging markets | | | | |
	MSEK	%	MSEK	%	MSEK	%	MSEK	%	%
Transport infrastructure	433	24	216	36	217	18	218	17	6
Roads and railways	(309)	(17)	(133)	(22)	(176)	(15)	(174)	(14)	--
Ports, airports, bridges	(124)	(7)	(83)	(14)	(41)	(3)	(44)	(3)	--
Telecommunication	324	18	38	6	286	24	309	24	41
Energy	314	18	22	4	292	25	299	23	23
Power and electricity	(180)	(10)	(2)	(0)	(178)	(15)	(180)	(14)	--
Hydro power	(72)	(4)	(0)	(0)	(72)	(6)	(72)	(6)	--
District heating	(62)	(4)	(20)	(4)	(42)	(4)	(47)	(4)	--
Water	155	9	63	11	92	8	94	7	9
Environment	85	5	44	7	41	3	46	3	
Buildings	145	8	104	18	41	3	44	3	8
Manufacturing	160	9	100	17	60	5	122	10	
Natural resources	79	4	2	0	77	7	76	6	0
Other sectors	93	5	9	1	84	7	84	7	13
All sectors	1,788	100	598	100	1,190	100	1,292	100	100

Note: All Swedish sales to growth markets are exports. The Norwegian figures are for 1995 when the total export was 717 MNOK. The Norwegian export in "other sectors" belongs to mountain plants and administration/operation (R.I.F., 1997).

Table A.5. Swedish, Norwegian and Danish exports by CFs across regions in 1996 in percent.

Region	Swedish	Norwegian	Danish
Nordic countries	4	3	33
Western Europe	3		
Other developed countries	3	0	0
Russia and Balticum	9	4	17
Central Europe	11		
Latin America	7	3	6
Africa	21	30	18
The Middle East	11	40	8
The Indian subcontinent	7	20	18
South-East Asia	22		
Eastern Asia	2		
All regions	100	100	100

Note: Total exports for Swedish CFs were 1,292 MSEK, for Norwegian CFs 717 MNOK (1995) and Danish CFs, here including architecture firms, around 1,300 MDKK (net sales). The Norwegian and Danish figures are taken from R.I.F. (1997) and F.R.I. (1997), respectively.

ments abroad (SKOL, 1997).

The high share of Africa for the Swedish and Norwegian CFs is partly explained by Sida's and NORAD's concentration of development assistance in Africa, but also by the expansion in the telecom sector—a sector where Sweden and Norway are strong—in this region. As late as 1991, the Danish CFs had 50% of their export to Africa, but a substantial reallocation has occurred toward Western, Central and Eastern Europe in recent years. Note also the Norwegian concentration in the Middle East, which is explained by large projects in the telecom sector. Swedish CFs seem to have problems in penetrating markets that earlier have been Spanish or French colonies because of language difficulties and Swedish CFs also perform weakly in Eastern Asia.

In emerging markets, the clients have mostly a low financial credibility, implying that the financing may be a problem for the exporting CFs. A large share of the assignments in these markets should rely on technical assistance and loans from development agencies. In Figure A.2, the exports by CFs to emerging

Figure A.2. Swedish, Norwegian and Danish exports to emerging markets by CFs distributed on financing in percent.

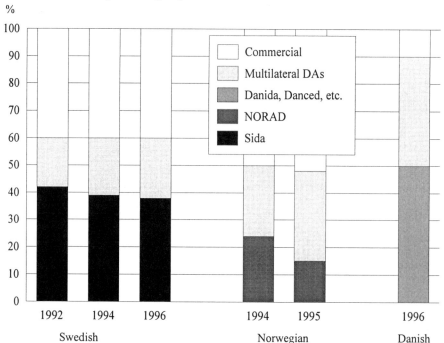

Note: The total Danish exports of 1,100 MDKK include only fees. Sida = Swedish International Development and Cooperation Agency. NORAD = Norwegian Agency for Development Cooperation. Danida = Danish International Development Assistance. DAs = development agencies. *Source*: IUI database, R.I.F. (1997) and F.R.I. (1997).

markets are distributed across financing alternatives. According to the firm-level survey, Sida financed assignments for 399 MSEK, 407 MSEK and 458 MSEK, respectively, in 1992, 1994 and 1996, whereas the corresponding figures for multilateral development agencies are 174 MSEK, 212 MSEK and 256 MSEK.[6] The shares on 40% and 20% for Sida and multilateral development agencies, respectively, seem to be stable, but these shares do not reflect the rapid expansion of Swedtel in the telecom sector, whose dependence on development agencies has decreased substantially during the period of measurement. Excluding Swedtel means that Sida accounted for 38%, 42% and 45% of the total export in 1992, 1994 and 1996, and multilateral development agencies had 18%, 23% and 26% of the total, significant increases in both cases. The awarded contracts

---

[6] Bilateral projects from other countries are not available for the CFs, because technical development assistance is tied in almost all OECD countries.

financed by multilateral development agencies are, however, concentrated to a few CFs.

For Norwegian CFs, commercial assignments also have a large share, which is explained by the dominance of Norconsult in the telecom sector. In absolute terms, NORAD financed assignments for 123 MNOK and 103 MNOK in 1994 and 1995. Corresponding figures for multilateral development agencies were 133 MNOK and 227 MNOK, respectively. In contrast, Danish CFs are 90% dependent on Danida (50%) and multilateral development agencies (40%). This figure reflects the fact that Danish CFs have a sector distribution other than what Swedish and Norwegian CFs have.

A.5 Statistics on Tender Documents

In this section, basic statistics on tender documents are described. First, I consider tender documents submitted abroad in competition, meaning that 358 of the 458 tender documents in the database are examined. The 100 negotiated contracts are presented separately at the end of the section. In Table A.6, the number of, and tender values of, awarded and lost tenders in competition are described across sectors. On average, the "success ratios" are 38% and 23%, respectively, for number of tenders and tender values.[7] This means that, awarded tenders, in general, are smaller than are lost tenders, which is explained by the fact that more tenderers choose to compete in order to use scope economies, or are allowed to compete, for large projects. For tender values, the success ratio is especially high in the district heating, building and natural resource sectors. This does not automatically mean that Swedish CFs have comparative advantages in these sectors. First, if Sida is often the financier or if the clients come from Sweden, then the success ratio is raised. The former is the case in the district heating sector, but Swedish clients are commonly in the building and manufacturing sectors. Second, a few large tenders on more than 30 MSEK can affect the success ratio for tender values considerably. This is the case in the water sector, where some lost tenders on 50 MSEK to 100 MSEK cause a large decrease in the success ratio. Therefore, one should also consider the success ratio for number of tenders when evaluating performance across sectors.

Awarded and lost tenders across regions are shown in Table A.7. The success ratios in developed markets are relatively high for tender values because the clients often are manufacturing firms, contractors or telecom operators

---

[7] As discussed in section A.1, these success ratios are somewhat overestimated but are not of great concern for the analysis as long as the overestimation is independent of the values of any other factors or variables.

Table A.6. Sample of awarded and lost tenders in competition for Swedish CFs across sectors between 1995 and 1997 in number, MSEK and percent.

Sector	Number of tenders				Tender values in MSEK			
	Won	Lost	All	% Won	Won	Lost	All	% Won
Roads and railways	19	42	61	31	64	356	420	15
Ports, airports and bridges	15	21	36	42	98	323	421	23
Telecom and other sectors	13	31	44	30	77	193	270	29
Power and electricity	12	24	36	33	30	197	227	13
Hydro power	6	11	17	35	56	294	350	16
District heating	15	15	30	50	33	51	84	39
Water	20	34	54	37	56	321	377	15
Environment	11	16	27	41	13	83	96	14
Buildings	5	12	17	29	64	82	146	44
Manufacturing	9	9	18	50	57	131	188	30
Natural resources	10	8	18	56	67	36	103	65
Total	135	223	358	38	615	2,067	2,682	23

Note: Negotiated contracts are excluded. Lost tenders have been more difficult to collect than awarded tenders. Therefore, the percentages of awarded tenders are somewhat overestimated. I do not expect, however, that this overestimation is systematic for any specific sector. Since the database is confidential and I do not wish to expose the success ratio of Swedtel, which dominates the telecom sector, I have chosen to combine the telecom and "other" sectors in one group. The number of tenders in other sectors is sufficiently high to keep Swedtel's success ratio a secret.

(Telia) that originate from Sweden. In the proposal database, such Swedish clients accounted for 46% of the awarded contract values in developed markets, whereas the corresponding figure for emerging markets was only 3%. For all tenders, developed markets account for 11% of the tender values, and Eastern Europe, Latin America, Africa and Asia stand for 21%, 9%, 16% and 43%, respectively. For awarded tenders, the distribution is approximately 12%, 21%, 15%, 21% and 30% for the five groups, implying that the success ratio is relatively low in Asia (compare with Table A.5).

Awarded and lost tenders as well as success ratios across financing groups are described in Table A.8. The success ratio for tender values is, of course, the

Table A.7. Sample of awarded and lost tenders in competition for Swedish CFs across regions between 1995 and 1997 in number, MSEK and percent.

Region	Number of tenders				Tender values in MSEK			
	Won	Lost	All	% Won	Won	Lost	All	% Won
Western Europe	10	15	25	40	45	184	229	20
Other developed countries	3	2	5	60	28	25	53	53
Central Europe	6	24	30	20	8	114	122	7
Baltic countries	21	36	57	37	62	134	196	32
Russia and Soviet countries	12	24	36	33	62	174	236	26
Latin America	15	13	28	54	95	159	254	37
Southern Africa	28	33	61	46	114	247	361	32
Northern Africa	5	8	13	38	15	44	59	25
The Middle East	5	14	19	26	64	323	387	17
The Indian subcontinent	6	12	18	33	12	304	316	4
South-East Asia	21	34	55	38	107	293	400	27
Eastern Asia	1	6	7	14	1	56	57	2
Regional	2	2	4	50	2	10	12	17
Total	135	223	358	38	615	2,067	2,682	23

Note: Negotiated contracts are excluded. It has been more difficult to collect lost tenders than awarded tenders. Therefore, the percentages of awarded tenders are somewhat overestimated. I do not expect, however, that this overestimation is systematic for any specific region.

highest for Sida-financed tenders, where seldom more than three tenderers participate. The share of awarded tenders is acceptably high for projects financed by EBRD and the World Bank as well as commercial tenders. For projects financed by Nordic funds and EU funds, the success ratios are 4% and 10%— not a very good performance by the Swedish CFs operating in the infrastructure sectors.

The distributions of tender values for all, awarded and lost tenders across financing groups are shown in Figure A.3. Of the awarded tenders, Sida dominates with about 42%, and multilateral and commercial projects account for 24% and 34%, respectively. These shares are not fully compatible with the shares in Figure A.2, because negotiated contracts are not included in Figure A.3.

Table A.8. Sample of awarded and lost tenders in competition for Swedish CFs across financing between 1995 and 1997 in number, MSEK and percent.

Financing group	Subgroup	Number of tenders				Tender values in MSEK			
		Won	Lost	All	%Won	Won	Lost	All	%Won
Sida		54	65	119	45	255.7	320.0	575.7	44
Nordic funds	NDF	0	4	4	0	0	80.8	80.8	0
	NEFCO	2	0	2	100	3.4	0	3.4	100
	Subtotal	2	4	6	33	3.4	80.8	84.2	4
EU funds	PHARE	7	20	27	26	18.7	93.3	112.0	17
	TACIS	0	10	10	0	0	119.0	119.0	0
	ALA	1	3	4	25	12.0	54.6	66.6	18
	Other	4	7	11	36	3.3	20.5	23.8	14
	Subtotal	12	40	52	23	34.0	287.4	321.4	11
EBRD		2	9	11	18	9.2	44.5	53.7	17
World Bank		8	22	30	27	60.7	226.6	287.3	21
Regional development banks	AsDB	8	16	24	33	24.7	152.1	176.8	14
	AfDB	1	2	3	33	4.0	13.0	17.0	24
	IDB	2	2	4	50	3.5	4.4	7.9	44
	Subtotal	11	20	31	35	32.2	169.5	201.7	16

Other	UN	5	2	7	71	4.2	3.4	7.6	55
	Other	5	8	13	38	7.8	62.8	70.6	11
	Subtotal	*10*	*10*	*20*	*50*	*12.0*	*66.2*	*78.2*	*15*
Commercial		*36*	*53*	*89*	*40*	*208.1*	*872.1*	*1080.2*	*19*
Total		135	223	358	38	615.3	2,067.1	2,682.4	23

Note: Negotiated contracts are excluded. It has been more difficult to collect lost tenders than awarded tenders. Therefore, the percentages of awarded tenders are somewhat overestimated. We do not expect, however, that this overestimation is systematic for any specific financing group.

Figure A.3. Distribution of tender values for all, awarded and lost tenders for Swedish CFs across financing between 1995 and 1997 in percent.

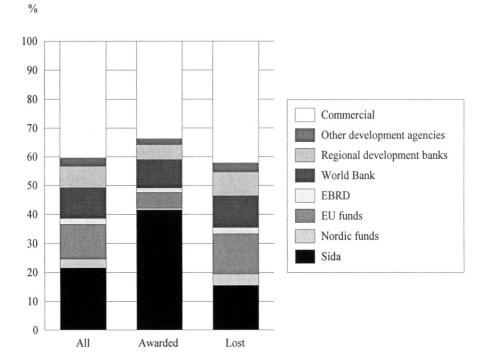

Now we turn to the negotiated tenders in the sample. Not surprisingly, 92 of 100 negotiations resulted in contracts for the Swedish CFs. For tender values, the awarded contracts account for 91% (176 of 193 MSEK). As can be seen in Table A.9, almost 50% of the negotiated contracts are financed by the clients. There is, however, a difference between new and continued contracts across financing alternatives. New contracts, which are not based on previous contracts for the client, are more frequent when the client finances the project himself, whereas continued contracts as a continuation of a previous contract are more frequent when development agencies are involved. This depends on the development agencies having strict rules for the maximum size of projects purchased through direct negotiations. Larger projects may only be negotiated as a continuation of previous contracts. Negotiations should be frequent when a specific CF already has executed services to a larger project. This supplier will then have information, and thereby cost, advantages compared to other competitors. Almost 50% of the project value of all negotiated contracts are continued contracts.

Although the negotiations are only 7% of the value of all tenders in the sample (193 divided by [193 plus 2,682]), negotiated contracts account for as

Table A.9. Negotiated contracts for Swedish CFs across financing groups between 1995 and 1997 in number and MSEK.

Financing group	Number of contracts			Contract values in MSEK		
	New	Continued	All	New	Continued	All
Sida	19	15	34	28.9	37.1	66.0
Other bilateral	1	0	1	12.0	0.0	12.0
World Bank	3	6	9	1.4	25.0	26.4
Other MDAs	3	2	5	0.5	3.3	3.8
Commercial	38	5	43	50.4	17.1	67.5
Total	64	28	92	93.2	82.5	175.7

Note: MDAs = multilateral development agencies.

much as 22% of the value of all awarded contracts (176 divided by [176 plus 615]). The distribution of negotiated contracts across sectors is shown in Table A.10. Such contracts are especially frequent in the roads and railways and telecom sectors. Also in this case, there is a large difference between new and continued contracts.

Negotiated contracts should occur when it is costly for the client to evaluate many proposals. If the evaluation is associated with some fixed costs, negotiations should be frequent when the contract value is low. As described in Table A.11, negotiated contracts are considerably smaller in contract value than are tenders in competition. The former contracts are only 1.9 MSEK on average where continued contracts are larger than new contracts across all financing groups. Tenders in competition have, on the other hand, an average size of 7.5 MSEK.

For both negotiated contracts and tenders in competition, projects financed by the World Bank are larger than projects financed by other development agencies. The World Bank finances to a higher degree projects associated with loans compared to other development agencies that give more technical assistance. It should, however, be noted that the tender values reflect only the value of the tenders for the firms in the sample and not for other international CFs that participate in the tenders. Joint ventures with other international CFs occur in 50% of all tenders in competition compared to 10% of all negotiated contracts. Joint ventures are especially frequent (more than 60%) when multilateral development agencies like the World Bank, regional development banks and EU funds are involved as financiers. The average value of the tenders in competition is therefore larger than 7.5 MSEK for all tenders and larger than 9.6 MSEK when the World Bank is financier.

Table A.10. Negotiated contracts for Swedish CFs across sectors between 1995 and 1997 in number and MSEK.

Sector	Number of contracts			Contract values in MSEK		
	New	Continued	All	New	Continued	All
Roads and railways	10	8	18	5.4	46.1	51.5
Ports, airports and bridges	5	1	6	22.7	4.5	27.2
Telecom and other sectors	5	2	7	32.1	9.0	41.1
Power and electricity	6	8	14	7.3	9.0	16.3
Hydro power	7	2	9	3.3	1.7	5.0
District heating	13	4	17	11.6	7.2	18.8
Water	10	1	11	4.5	0.2	4.7
Environment	3	0	3	4.3	0.0	4.3
Buildings	2	0	2	0.8	0.0	0.8
Manufacturing	3	0	3	1.2	0.0	1.2
Natural resources	0	2	2	0.0	4.8	4.8
Total	64	28	92	93.2	82.5	175.7

Table A.11. Average size of negotiated contracts and tenders in competition in MSEK.

Financing group	Negotiated contracts			Tenders in competition		
	New	Continued	All	Won	Lost	All
Sida	1.5	2.5	1.9	4.7	4.9	4.8
World Bank	0.5	4.2	2.9	7.6	10.3	9.6
Other MDAs	0.2	1.6	0.8	2.5	7.8	6.2
Commercial	1.3	3.4	1.6	5.8	16.5	12.1
Total	1.5	2.9	1.9	4.6	9.3	7.5

Note: MDAs = multilateral development agencies. The tender values reflect only the value of the contract for the tendering firm in the sample. If the tendering firm has a joint venture with another international CF, the contract value for the latter firm is not included in the figures.

Appendix B

QUESTIONNAIRES

B.1 Questionnaire on Firms

Swedish consulting firm's international operations
Confidential

Name of the firm			
Contact person			
Telephone, fax and e-mail			

1. The firm's **total sales**, **foreign sales** and **exports from Sweden, 1992, 1994** and **1996**. With foreign sales means external turnover abroad, that is, including exports from Sweden but excluding exports of foreign offices to Sweden. The cells A, B and C are divided in coming questions. Emerging markets comprise both developing countries and Eastern Europe.

	MSEK 1992	MSEK 1994	MSEK 1996
(a) Total sales.			
(b) Foreign sales	(A)	(B)	(C)
(c) **of which** in developed countries			(G)
(d) **of which** in emerging markets.	(J)	(K)	(L)
(e) Exports from Sweden	(D)	(E)	(F)
(f) **of which** to developed countries			(H)
(g) **of which** to emerging markets.			(M)

2. The firm's **number of employees**. Average number of employees in each year.	Number 1992	Number 1994	Number 1996
(a) in Sweden.			
(b) in other developed countries			
(c) in emerging markets.			

3. The firm's **foreign sales** and **exports** divided by **region**.	Foreign sales MSEK 1996	Exports MSEK 1996
Nordic countries (excluding Sweden)		
Western Europe (excluding Nordic countries)		
North America (USA and Canada)		
Japan, Australia and New Zealand		
Totals for developed countries	(G)	(H)
Russia and former Soviet countries (including Balticum)		
Central Europe (Poland, Czech Rep., Slovakia, Romania, Bulgaria,Yugoslavia, Bosnia, Croatia, Macedonia and Albania)		
Latin America		
Africa		
Eastern Asia (China PR, Hong Kong, Taiwan, Korea)		
South-East Asia (Thailand, Burma, Malaysia, Vietnam, Singapore, Laos, Campuchea, Indonesia, Philippines)		
The Indian subcontinent (India, Sri Lanka, Pakistan, Bangladesh)		
The Middle East (Iran, Israel and the Asian Arab countries)		
Totals for emerging markets	(L)	(M)
Totals (will correspond to cells C and F in question 1)	(C)	(F)

4. The firm's **foreign sales in emerging markets** divided by **financing group**. Make reasonable estimates.	MSEK		
	1992	1994	1996
Multilateral development agencies (World Bank, AsDB, EBRD, EU funds, etc.)			
Bilateral development agencies			
of which Swedish bilateral development agencies			
Commercial projects			
Totals (will correspond to cells J, K and L in question 1)	(J)	(K)	(L)

5. The firm's **foreign sales** and **exports** in **developed countries** and **emerging markets** divided by **sector**.	MSEK 1996			
	Developed countries		Emerging markets	
	Foreign sales	Exports	Foreign sales	Exports
Transport infrastructure (roads, railways, bridges, airports, harbors, etc.)				
Telecommunication				
Energy (power, electricity, hydro power, district heating, etc.)				
Manufacturing (industrial plants and process systems)				
Natural resources (mining, gas, oil, agriculture, forestry, etc.)				
Water (water supply and waste water)				
Environment (waste, environmental control, etc.)				
Buildings (residential blocks, hospitals, offices, etc.)				
Other sectors (government administration, health, etc.)				
Totals (will correspond to G, H, J and K in question 1)	(G)	(H)	(J)	(K)

6. The firm's **market observation of foreign markets**. Make reasonable estimates.	Percent 1996
Contacts with old clients or via own local offices	
Via other, Swedish or international, consulting firms	
Via local consulting firms or contact persons	
Via contractors	
Via development agencies (Sida, World Bank, AsDB, EBRD, EU funds, UN, etc.)	
Other ways (export-promoting organizations or Ministry of Foreign Affairs, etc.)	
Total	100 %

B.2 Questionnaire on Proposals

Swedish consulting firm's foreign proposals 1995-97
Confidential
One questionnaire for each foreign proposal.

1. Name of the firm	2. Name of the project	3. Year	4. Host country
		199	

5. The firm has **previously had projects in the host country**	Yes		No	

6. (a) **Orderer** of the project (Note! Does **not** need to be **financier**). Mark with **one** X.	From the host country		From Sweden	From other country
	Private	Govern-mental		
Client				
Contractor				
(b) The firm has **previously had contracts for the orderer**.	Yes		No	
(c) The firm **visited the orderer** in connection with the tender.	Yes		No	

7. (a) **Financing** of the project. Mark with **one** X.			
Sida (including other Swedish financiers)			
Multilateral development agencies (**state which ones**)			
Commercial project			
(b) The firm has **previously had this kind of financing**.	Yes		No	

8. The project concerned is a **physical investment project**.	Yes		No	

| 9. **Tasks** in the project. Mark with **one or several** X's. | Project management | |
	Supervision of contractor	
Master plan	Commissioning	
Feasibility study	Training	
Preliminary design	Other study or investigation (not feasibility study)	
Detailed design	Institutional building	
Procurement	Administration or operator services	

10. **Sector** of the project. Mark with **one** X.					
Transport infrastructure		Energy		Natural resources	
Telecommunication		Buildings		Manufacturing	
Water and waste water		Environment		Other sectors	

11. **The firm's international experience** of *similar* projects during the last 10 years. Number of contracts.	No	1-5	6-10	11-20	>20

12. (a) The firm's **team leader** for the project.				
(b) The team leader's **international experience. Number of years** abroad.	0-2	2-5	5-10	>10
(c) The team leader's **formal education**.	Secondary school	University	Licentiate	Doctor

13. The firm's **status**/planned status in the project. Mark with **one** cross.							
Alone		Head consultant		Joint venture		Subconsultant	

14. The firm (planned) to cooperate with	Yes	No
(a) **contractors** (from any country)		
(b) other **Swedish or international consulting firms**		
(c) **local consulting firms**.		
(d) State the **local consultants'** (planned) **volume share** (man months) in the project. (Note! **Not invoicing share**). Make a reasonable estimate.		%

15. **Tender system.** Mark with **one** X.	Open tender		
	Competitive tender with invitation or short-listing		
	Negotiated contract (no competition)	New project	
		Continued project	

16. The firm won the tender.	Yes		No	

17. **Contract value** of the project (including reimbursements).		MSEK

REFERENCES

Aharoni, Y. (ed.), 1993, *Coalitions and Competition: The Globalization of Professional Services*, London: Routledge.

Andersson, T., T. Fredriksson and R. Svensson, 1996, *Multinational Restructuring, Internationalization and Small Economies: The Swedish Case*, London: Routledge.

Arrow, K.J., 'The Economic Implications of Learning by Doing', *Review of Economic Studies*, 29: 155-73.

AsDB, 1997, 1998a, *Annual reports 1997 and 1998*, Manila: Asian Development Bank.

AsDB, 1998b, Unpublished data, Manila: Asian Development Bank.

Bergquist, A., 1993, *Sveriges internationella handel med tjänster*, Licentiate thesis, Lund: Department of Economics, Lund University.

Danida, 1998, *Annual report 1998*, Copenhagen: Danida.

Dunning, J., 1977, 'Location of Economic Activities and the MNE: A Search for an Eclectic Approach', in B. Ohlin, P.-O. Hesselborn and P.-M. Wijkman (eds.), *The Allocation of International Production: Proceedings of a Nobel Symposium in Stockholm*, London: MacMillan.

EFCA, 1997, 'Standardization in Procedures for the Engagement of Consultants', *Euro News*, june 1997, Brussels: EFCA.

F.R.I., 1997, Rådgivende ingeniører: Statistisk branschebeskrivelse 1997, Copenhagen: Føreningen af Rådgivende Ingeniører (F.R.I.).

Grönroos, C., 1990, *Service Management and Marketing*, Lexington, Mass.: Lexington Books.

Hansen, M.T., N. Nohria and T. Tierney, 1999, 'What's Your Strategy for Managing Knowledge?', *Harvard Business Review*, March-April, 106-16.

Johanson, J. and D.D. Sharma, 1983, 'The Foreign Operations of Swedish Technical Consultancy Firms: An Empirical Study', CIF Working paper 1983/5, Uppsala: Uppsala University.

Johanson, J. and D.D. Sharma, 1984, 'Swedish Technical Consultants: Tasks, Resources and Relationships—A Network Approach', CIF Working paper 1984/5, Uppsala: Uppsala University.

Johanson, J. and J.E.Vahlne, 1977, 'The Internationalization Process of the Firm—A Model of Knowledge Development and Increasing Foreign Market Commitments', *Journal of International Business Studies*, 8: 23-32.

Lageson, P., 1999, *The Purchasing of Technical Consultancy Services. A Case Study of Buyer-Seller Relationships*, Licentiate thesis, Luleå: Luleå University of Technology, Department of Business Administration and Social Science.

Løwendahl, B.R., 1997, *Strategic Management of Professional Service Firms*, Copenhagen: Copenhagen Business School Press.

Maula, M., 1999, *Multinational Companies as Learning and Evolution Systems. A Multi-Case Study of Knowledge-Intensive Service Companies. An Application of Autopoiesis Theory*, Ph.D. thesis, Helsingfors: Helsinki School of Economics and Business Administration.

Mytelka, L., 1985, 'Stimulating Effective Technology: The Case of Textiles in Africa', in N. Rosenberg and C. Frischtak (eds.), *International Technology Transfer: Concepts, Measures and Comparisons*, New York: Praeger.

NDF, 1999, Unpublished data, Helsingfors: Nordic Development Fund.

Nielsen, N.C., 1996, 'The Concept of Technological Service Infrastructures: Innovation and the Creation of Good Jobs', in OECD documents, *Employment and Growth in the Knowledge-Based Economy*, Paris: OECD.

Niosi, J., P. Hanel and L. Fizet, 1995, 'Technology Transfer to Developing Countries through Engineering Firms: The Canadian Experience', *World Development*, 23: 1815-24.

Ordover, J.A. and G. Saloner, 1989, 'Predation, Monopolization and Antitrust', in R. Schmalensee and R.D. Willig (eds.), *Handbook of Industrial Organization*, Vol. 1, Amsterdam: North-Holland.

Rada, J., 1987, 'Information Technology and Services', in O. Giarini, (ed.), *The Eemerging Service Economy*, Oxford: Pergamon Press.

R.I.F., 1997, Unpublished data, Oslo: Rådgivende Ingeniørers Forening (R.I.F.).

Roberts, J., 1972, 'Engineering Consultancy, Industrialization and Development', *Journal of Development Studies*, 9: 39-61.

Sapir, A., 1990, 'The Structure of Service in Europe. A Conceptual Framework'. Discussion Paper No. 498, London: CEPR.

Scherer, F., 1986, On the Current State of Knowledge, in H. de Jong and W. Shepard (eds.), *Mainstreams in Industrial Organisation*, Dordrecht: Martinus Nijhoff Publishers.

Seymour, H., 1987, *The Multinational Construction Industry*, London: Croom Helm.

Sharma, D.D. and J. Johanson, 1987, 'Technical Consultancy in Internationalization', *International Marketing Review*, 4: 20-29.

Sharma, D.D. and R. Keller, 1993, 'Exporting in a Network: Relationship between Technical Consultancy and the Sources of Procurement', in D.D. Sharma (ed.), *Industrial Networks. Advances in International Marketing*, Connecticut: JAI Press Inc.

Sida, 1997, Unpublished data, Stockholm: Sida.

Sida, 1998, *Annual report 1998*, Stockholm: Sida.

Sida, 1999a, Unpublished data on Sida's budget distributed on implementing organizations, Stockholm: Sida.

Sida, 1999b, Unpublished data on tender evaluations, Stockholm: Sida.

Siggel, E., 1986, 'Technology Transfers to Developing Countries through Consulting Engineers: A Model and Empirical Observations from Canada', *Developing Economies*, 24: 229-50.

SKOL, 1997, Unpublished data, Espo: The Finnish Association of Consulting firms (SKOL)

Stewart, C.T. and Y. Nihei, 1987, *Technology Transfer and Human Factors*, Lexington, MA: Heath & Co.

Swedish Delegation at European Union, 1999, Unpublished data, Brussels: Swedish Delegation at European Union.

Swedish Federation of Architects and Consulting Engineers, 1998, *Branschöversikt*, january 1998, Stockholm.

Svenska Konsultföreningen, 1982, *Den svenska tekniska konsultbranschen*, Stockholm: Svenska Konsultföreningen.

Svensson, R., 1996, *Svenska företags projektverksamhet i utlandet*, Stockholm: International Council of Swedish Industry (NIR).

Svensson, R., 1997, *Svenska tekniska konsulters tjänsteexport: Investerings-projekt, teknologi och biståndsfinansiering*, Stockholm: Sida.

Svensson, R., 1998, 'Exporting Consultancy Services in the Infrastructure Sectors: The Determinants of Obtaining Asignments', Working Paper No. 508, Stockholm: The Research Institute of Industrial Economics (IUI).

Svensson, R., 1999, *Visits to the Client when Tendering for Consulting Contracts: Sourcing Information or Affecting the Client?*, Discussion paper, Stockholm: The Research Institute of Industrial Economics (IUI).

Taxell, P., 1996, *Andra länders bilaterala bistånd—en finansieringskälla för svensk utlandsexport?*, PUG 1996:3, Stockholm: Ministry of Foreign Affairs.

Teece, D., 1981, 'The Market for Know-How and the International Transfer of Technology', *The Annuals, Association of Political and Social Sciences*, No. 458, November.

Tirole, J., 1986, *The Theory of Industrial Organization*, Cambridge: MIT Press.

Tordoir, P., 1995, *The Professional Knowledge Economy: The Management and Integration of Professional Services in Business Organizations*, Boston: Kluwer Academic Publishers.

UN, 1997, *1996 International Trade Statistics Yearbook*, New York: United Nations.

UN, 1998, *World Investment Report 1998: Trends and Determinants*, New York and Geneva: United Nations.

Wikström, S. and R. Normann, 1994, *Knowledge & Value—A New Perspective on Corporate Transformation*, London: Routledge.

Williamson, O., 1989, 'Transaction Cost Economics', in R.Schmalensee and R.D. Willig (eds.), *Handbook of Industrial Organization*, Amsterdam: North-Holland.

World Bank, 1997, 1998a, *Annual reports 1997 and 1998*, New York, World Bank.

World Bank, 1998b, *World Development Indicators*, database, World Bank.

ABBREVIATIONS

ÅF	Ångpanneföreningen (Swedish CF)
AfDB	African Development Bank
AsDB	Asian Development Bank
CF	consulting firm
Danida	Danish International Development Assistance
DA	development agency
EBRD	European Bank for Reconstruction and Development
EFCA	European Federation of Engineering Consultancy Associations
EU-ALA	EU fund for Asia and Latin America
EU-PHARE	EU fund for Central Europe and Balticum
EU-TACIS	EU fund for former Soviet-countries and Mongolia
Finnida	Finnish International Development Agency
FVB	Fjärrvärmebyrån (Swedish CF)
IBRD	International Bank for Reconstruction and Development
IDA	International Development Association
IDB	Inter-American Development Bank
IFC	International Finance Corporation
IUI	The Research Institute of Industrial Economics
J&W	Jacobson & Widmark (Swedish CF)
KM	Kjessler & Mannerstråhle (Swedish CF)
LTR	long-term relationship
MDA	multilateral development agency
NCG	Nordic Consulting Group (Nordic CF)
NDF	Nordic Development Fund
NEFCO	Nordic Environment Finance Corporation
NGO	nongovernmental organization
NORAD	Norwegian Agency for Development Cooperation
OECD	Organization for Economic Cooperation and Development
R&D	research and development
SCC	Scandiaconsult (Swedish CF)
SGAB	Swedish Geological AB (Swedish CF)
Sida	Swedish International Development and Cooperation Agency
TCF	technical consulting firm
UN	United Nations
WB	World Bank

INDEX

Economics of Science, Technology and Innovation

18. J. S. Metcalfe and I. Miles (eds.):
    Innovation Systems in the Service Economy:
    Measurement and Case Study Analysis   ISBN 0-7923-7730-3
19. R. Svensson:
    Success Strategies and Knowledge Transfer in
    Cross-Border Consulting Operations   ISBN 0-7923-7776-1

KLUWER ACADEMIC PUBLISHERS — BOSTON / DORDRECHT / LONDON